The Yangtze

Titles in the Rivers of the World series include:

RIVERS
of the
WORLD

The Yangtze

James Barter

LUCENT
BOOKS

THOMSON
—★—
™
GALE

San Diego • Detroit • New York • San Francisco • Cleveland • New Haven, Conn. • Waterville, Maine • London • Munich

THOMSON

─────✳─────™

GALE

© 2003 by Lucent Books. Lucent Books is an imprint of The Gale Group, Inc., a division of Thomson Learning, Inc.

Lucent Books® and Thomson Learning™ are trademarks used herein under license.

For more information, contact
Lucent Books
27500 Drake Rd.
Farmington Hills, MI 48331-3535
Or you can visit our Internet site at http://www.gale.com

LIBRARY OF CONGRESS CATALOGING-IN-PUBLICATION DATA

Barter, James, 1946–
    The Yangtze / by James Barter.
       p. cm. — (Rivers of the world)
Includes bibliographical references and index.
Summary: Discusses the early Yangtze, the river as a lifeline for China, and conservation and development of the river.
    ISBN 1-59018-370-3 (hardback : alk. paper)
   1. Yangtze River (China)—Juvenile literature. [1. Yangtze River (China)] I. Title. II.
Rivers of the world (Lucent Books)
    DS793 .Y3B37 2003
    951'.2—dc21

                                2002154434

Printed in the United States of America

Contents

• • • • • • • • • • • • •

Foreword

· · · · · · · · · · · ·

Human history and rivers are inextricably intertwined. Of all the geologic wonders of nature, none has played a more central and continuous role in the history of civilization than rivers. Fanning out across every major landmass except the Antarctic, all great rivers wove an arterial network that played a pivotal role in the inception of early civilizations and in the evolution of today's modern nation-states.

More than ten thousand years ago, when nomadic tribes first began to settle into small, stable communities, they discovered the benefits of cultivating crops and domesticating animals. These incipient civilizations developed a dependence on continuous flows of water to nourish and sustain their communities and food supplies. As small agrarian towns began to dot the Asian and African continents, the importance of rivers escalated as sources of community drinking water, as places for washing clothes, for sewage removal, for food, and as means of transportation. One by one, great riparian civilizations evolved whose collective fame is revered today, including ancient Mesopotamia, between the Tigris and Euphrates Rivers; Egypt, along the Nile; India, along the Ganges and Indus Rivers; and China, along the Yangtze. Later, for the same reasons, early civilizations in the Americas gravitated to the major rivers of the New World such as the Amazon, Mississippi, and Colorado.

For thousands of years, these rivers admirably fulfilled their role in nature's cycle of birth, death, and renewal. The waters also supported the rise of nations and their expanding populations. As hundreds and then thousands of cities sprang up along major rivers, today's modern nations emerged and discovered modern uses for the rivers. With more mouths to feed than ever before, great irrigation canals supplied by river water fanned out across the landscape, transforming parched land into mile upon mile of fertile cropland. Engineers developed the mathematics needed to throw great concrete dams across rivers to control occasional flooding and to store trillions of gallons of water to irrigate crops during the hot summer months. When the great age of electricity arrived, engineers added to the demands placed on rivers by using their cascading water to drive huge hydroelectric turbines to light and heat homes and skyscrapers in urban settings. Rivers also played a major role in the development of modern factories as sources of water for processing a variety of commercial goods and as a convenient place to discharge various types of refuse.

For a time, civilizations and rivers functioned in harmony. Such a benign relationship, however, was not destined to last. At the end of the twentieth century, scientists confirmed the opinions of environmentalists: The viability of all major rivers of the world was threatened. Urban populations could no longer drink the fetid water, masses of fish were dying from chemical toxins, and microorganisms critical to the food chain were disappearing along with the fish species at the top of the chain. The great hydroelectric dams had altered the natural flow of rivers, blocking migratory fish routes. As the twenty-first century unfolds, all who have contributed to spoiling the rivers are now in agreement that immediate steps must be taken to heal the rivers if their partnership with civilization is to continue.

Each volume in the Lucent Rivers of the World series tells the unique and fascinating story of a great river and its people. The significance of rivers to civilizations is emphasized to highlight both their historical role and the present situation. Each volume illustrates the idiosyncrasies of one great river in terms of its physical attributes, the plants and animals that depend on it, its role in ancient and modern cultures, how it served the needs of the people, the misuse of the river, and steps now being taken to remedy its problems.

Introduction

· · · · · · · · · · · · · · · · ·

A Dragon of a River

The Yangtze is a dragon of a river—serpentine, deadly, reluctant to be tamed. For eons before the first primitive villages grew up close to its banks, the Yangtze had been flowing east from the snowcapped mountains of Tibet to the East China Sea. This mighty river gains speed from a twenty-two-thousand-foot vertical drop, gathers heft from seven hundred tributaries, and cuts across all of China, dividing the predominantly wheat-eating north from the rice-eating south. The fickle Yangtze turns especially treacherous as it slams through a string of narrow gorges, "Like a thousand seas poured into one cup,"[1] wrote the twelfth-century poet Su Dongpo.

For hundreds of generations, no one could have imagined that this mighty dragon could ever be tamed. Yet within the past fifty years, a mere tick on the clock measuring the life of the Yangtze, political and social events within China have altered the river in ways that would make it unrecognizable to earlier generations. Some view these changes as a great leap forward for all of China while others believe they are actually witnessing a great leap back.

In 1949, amidst growing sentiment to effect significant change in China, a political revolution swept across the country. In the ensuing years, the Yangtze River played a major role in the development of China's new economy. As the country's major river system, the Yangtze and its vast network of tributaries extend far into China's interior and

The mighty Yangtze is China's most celebrated river, stretching nearly four thousand miles from east to west.

became the home for thousands of factories, both large and small, that use Yangtze water for processing goods and as a sewer for discarding toxic effluents. As China's largest waterway, the river experiences large cargo barges laden with agricultural and manufactured goods. And as China's largest source of irrigation water, the Yangtze was rerouted to dryer northern provinces by dams which also generate hydroelectricity to power the factories and large cities new to the banks of the river.

As a major role player in China's new economy, the Yangtze is a colossal success. However, there was a terrible price paid. No longer does a mighty healthy river flow through a bucolic land of mountains, forests, and farmlands. The taming of the dragon has placed a shroud of pollution throughout the river and its habitat. Chinese officials aware of the problems have pledged billions of dollars to clean and restore the river to its former health and remain optimistic that a cure can be found. Scientists and environmentalists outside of China, however, have their doubts about these pledges, believing that such promises are too small and too late to return the river to its former health.

1
· · · · · · · · · ·

Carver of Mountains

The Yangtze is the longest, largest, and most celebrated river in China. Called simply *Changjiang* (Long River) by the Chinese, it spans nine provinces for a distance of thirty-nine hundred miles. The name is an apt description of the longest river in China and the third longest in the world after the Nile in Africa and the Amazon in South America. Among the great powerful rivers of the world, the Yangtze is unique because it sliced most of its path to the sea through one rugged mountain range after another, earning it the name "Carver of Mountains."

The cutting edge of this thunderous knife is its astonishing volume of water—it outputs 1.244 trillion cubic yards annually—second only to the Amazon. Such a volume surging down and across the Chinese landscape for millions of years has shaped the river's general east-west axis. It is recognized by the Chinese people as the country's natural dividing line defining the north and south.

The river is so large and spans so many regions that within China it has acquired a handful of colorful local names. High in the Qinghai-Tibet plateau near its headwaters, local tribes call it *Dri Chu* meaning Female Yak River. Villagers living south of the plateau know it as *Tongtian He*, Traveling-Through-the-Heavens River. Where it borders the Sichuan (Szechwan) and runs through the Yunnan Provinces, it is referred to as *Jinsha*, River of Golden Sand. It is only the last three- or four-hundred mile section that is known to Chinese as the Yangtze. The first westerners who

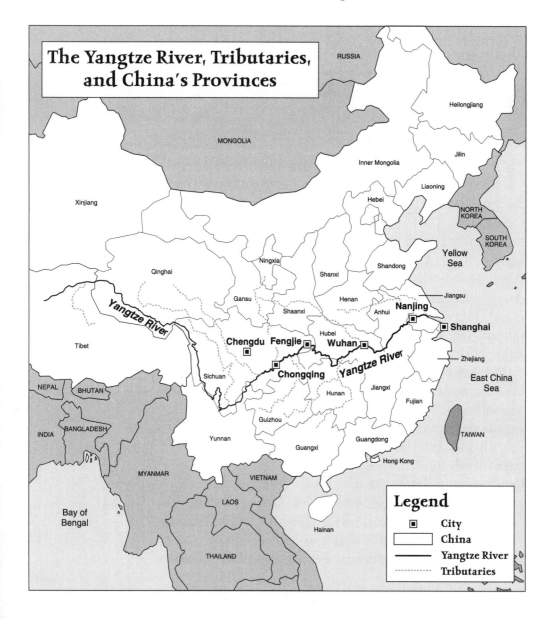

A Chinese fisherman fixes his net in the Yangtze swollen with rains. During the monsoon season, the Yangtze is highly prone to flooding.

entered the Yangtze sailed only a few hundred miles upriver from the Pacific Coast. For this reason, they mistakenly thought that its name, the Yangtze, applied to the entire river's length, and foreigners came to recognize the entire river as the Yangtze.

A satellite photograph mapping of the Yangtze River basin reveals much about the great river's character. Brown and ice-gray terrain close to its source reveals a barren and harsh environment until it reaches further south. There the photograph reveals a thin yet rich green vegetation band along the riverbanks as it winds its way through a series of tightly clustered mountain ranges for more than a thousand miles. As the river slices its way east, the vegetation band widens a bit and then dramatically fans out at the Yangtze

Delta, one of the most fertile zones in the world, near its confluence with the East China Sea. Along this path, the river and its tributaries drain an area of about 760,000 square miles, equivalent to 20 percent of China's total land mass and home to 400 million Chinese, roughly one-third of the entire population.

The Yangtze's surge is predictable and mild during the cold winters but becomes monstrous and unpredictable during the summer months. When the summer sun warms the air, monsoon conditions sweep across the Yangtze basin occasionally dropping torrential downpours of two to three feet of rain in a single week, causing flash floods. As this enormous volume of water cascades uncontrollably down the mountains throughout the southern provinces, a network of hundreds of tributaries capture the barrage and carry it inexorably toward the Yangtze. As the tributaries feed into the main trunk of the river, the Yangtze becomes a wall of water crashing through gorges and canyons on its dash to the sea. When this cresting torrent reaches the river's mouth, it expels as much as 6 billion cubic yards of water a day across the low-lying delta, driving its muddy brown water a hundred miles out to sea.

The immense Yangtze River basin is divided into three zones called reaches: the upper, middle, and lower. Each reach has a unique geological and meteorological signature that collectively defines the river's personality.

Upper Reach: Mountains Upon Mountains

The Upper Reach of the Yangtze, the longest of the three reaches, runs twenty-seven hundred miles from its source high up in the Tibetan plateau in Qinghai Province to the city of Yichang in Sichuan Province. This section of the basin is geographically distinguished by having the source of the Yangtze and by its rugged mountain terrain. It is along this reach that the Yangtze takes a precipitous drop in elevation that accounts for 95 percent of its total descent as its very narrow route slices through the mountainous countryside.

The great river begins its long trek to the sea as a modest stream of pure sparkling glacial water. This water issues forth from two glaciers high up in the Tanggula

In Search of the Yangtze Headwaters

Finding the headwaters of the Yangtze had long been a geographical conundrum. The Tibetan plateau, a forbidding and inhospitable wind-swept terrain, was visited by few people before the nineteenth century. The difficulty of climbing to the mountain ranges on this plateau guarded the Yangtze's secret in spite of several attempts to locate the source.

According to the earliest known treatise written sometime between 478 and 221 B.C., the Mingshan Mountains in Sichuan Province was the source—an error of more than a thousand miles. It was not until more than two thousand years later in the sixteenth century that explorers recognized that the source had to be in Qinghai Province. They determined that the Jinsha River was the source. This was an enormous correction over the previous determination but it was not until the eighteenth century that explorers sent by the government narrowed the search to the Tibetan plateau.

During the 1970s expeditions of scientists trudged up to the Tibetan plateau and narrowed their search to the Tanggula mountain range. Loaded with precise measuring devices they discovered forty active glaciers spawning streams and 149 snowcapped peaks, twenty of which were over twenty thousand feet, with rivulets emanating from all of them. By using their instrumentation and the process of elimination, they found a small stream active all year long coming from Mount Geladandong, even though it was not the tallest of the many peaks in the range. Scaling the peak, the team came upon two tongue-shaped glaciers close together, each six miles long and one mile wide. As the team began examining the melt from the two tongues of ice, they realized that the rivulets of pristine ice water joined together not more than a mile from the glaciers to start their descent down Mount Geladandong that would eventually reach the East China Sea. They had discovered the ultimate source of the Yangtze.

Mountains on the Tibetan plateau of western central China. It was not until 1976 that the true source of the Yangtze was determined to be these glaciers on the twenty-two-thousand-foot-high Mount Geladandong. From its glacial origins, for the first forty miles the shallow river flows east, filling the broad plain with ever-shifting braids of icy water small enough for yaks, donkeys, and other local animals to wade across. It is then joined by many other rivulets that flow for another five hundred miles, first continuing east and then abruptly south through highlands of sparse barley fields where hardy Tibetan herdsmen live in yakskin tents called *yurts*.

At the city of Qumarleb, the Yangtze takes the local name, the Jinsha River, the River of Golden Sand. Here the river contains just enough gold flakes to be slightly noticeable, which gives this section of the Yangtze its name. As the river flows south through desolate yet beautiful land forms, it reaches the southern edge of the Tibetan plateau, where it plunges off what the locals call the "Roof of the World" through a series of deep ravines and gorges.

For the next twelve hundred miles, the river forms the border between China and Tibet. On its southward trek, the river comes to the city of Shigu, meaning Stone Drum, and makes an abrupt U-turn north so dramatically that it actually runs parallel to itself, separated by only fourteen miles. This famous turn, known as the First Bend, provides some of the finest alpine scenery on the river.

Twenty miles downstream from the First Bend is an equally spectacular site. A canyon, ten miles long but narrowing at one point to a mere forty-five feet, appears to have been sliced through the mountains with the blade of a giant knife. This is Hutiao Canyon, meaning Tiger's leap, so named because local legend tells the story of a great tiger that once made the leap across. After a hundred miles flowing due north, the river makes a second bend and abruptly turns back south again until it reaches its southernmost city, Longjie, where it commences its northeast journey to the sea.

As the river moves north through the province of Sichuan, meaning Four Rivers, the now mighty Yangtze picks up the flow of four major tributaries as it continues to carve its riverbed deep through the rugged terrain. As the river flows through the gorges, it etches its way through the mud and rock mountainsides picking up minerals in the form of silt that will later fertilize valley vegetation downriver.

For hundreds of miles, peaks rise thousands of feet above the river far below. Ancient peoples strung single rope bridges from canyon side to canyon side, their only means of crossing the swirling rapids below. A single rider was placed in a wicker cage attached to a pulley greased with yak butter to reduce friction on the rope.

The Three River Gorges

When the Yangtze reaches the city of Fengjie, it enters the most famous and most dramatic stretch of the river. For one hundred and fifty miles the river flows through three gorges that are collectively called the *Sanxia*, or Three Gorges: the Qutang, Wushan, and Xiling. These three gorges function as a check on the enormous volume of water along the upper reach. Structurally they are very much like the narrow neck of an hourglass; wide at each end but constricted in the center. During floods, when enormous volumes of water are obstructed by the narrows, the river rises hundreds of feet, scouring the hillsides of mud, rock, trees, and often entire villages.

As the Yangtze surges downstream, the valley begins to narrow at the five-mile-long Qutang Gorge, meaning Wind Box Gorge, the shortest and most dramatic of the gorges; its widest point is a mere five hundred feet. Its Mesozoic limestone peaks, which were formed during the period of the dinosaurs about 100 million years ago, tower over four thousand feet above the river. The vertical cliffs are adorned with ancient stairs and paths that fuel tales of great generals and civil wars fought above the raging Yangtze. In 1170 the poet Lu You described this awe-inspiring gorge:

A tourist cruise liner navigates between the towering cliffs of Fengjie's Qutang Gorge. The gorge is a popular part of any tourist trip along the Yangtze.

Entering the Qutang Gorge, I saw two rocky walls rising into the clouds and facing each other across the river. They were as smooth as if they had been cut with an axe. I raised my head and looked up. The sky was like a narrow waterfall. But there was no water falling down. The river in the gorge was as smooth as shining oil.[2]

Just below Qutang is the entrance to the second gorge. Stretching twenty-five miles, Wushan, meaning Witches

Gorge, is situated between Sichuan and Hubei Provinces. The gorge is most noted for its twelve sculpted peaks. The most geologically interesting of the peaks is Goddess Peak because it resembles the figure of a kneeling maiden. It is said that the peak is an embodiment of Yao Ji, one of the daughters of the Queen Mother of the West, a folk figure imbued with many charming and elegant attributes. Local legend has it that after returning from her travels from the East Sea, Yao Ji stumbled upon twelve dragons that were wreaking havoc on the river and mountains, leaving a deluge of floods and destruction in their wake. She resigned herself and her eleven maidens to the tallest peak, Goddess Peak, in order to protect the boatmen and peasants whose lives were intertwined with the river.

The third and final gorge, Xiling, extends for forty-seven miles. This is the most violent stretch of the Yangtze. Enormous boulders lie just below the surface of the water making the river a swirling death trap for boaters during periods of low water. In a two-mile section of white-water fury, the water elevation abruptly drops twenty feet. A shrine called the "White Bone Pagoda" once stood here on the river's bank, so named because a giant pile of bleached bones was all that remained of hundreds of voyagers killed at this spot.

Finally, after twenty-seven hundred miles, the Yangtze eases into the city of Yichang, marking the end of the upper reach and the beginning of the middle reach. At an elevation of only eleven hundred feet, the Yangtze changes its personality from a river of unrestrained fury slicing through narrow gorges to one of placid and slow-flowing serenity. From Yichang to the East China Sea, the river's drop in elevation is a mere one foot per mile over its last twelve hundred miles.

Middle Reach

Yichang marks many beginnings. It is this segment of the river that Chinese maps refer to as the *Changjiang*. More importantly, it is here that the river ceases its dramatic plunge from its source as it abruptly emerges from mountainous gorges, slowing and widening enough to accommodate navigation of large cargo ships. The significance of the slowing and broadening of the river cannot be underestimated. This is the first reach of the river where farmers are able to use the river's water and nutrient-rich silt needed for their grain harvests.

This six-hundred-mile-long middle reach of the Yangtze basin is centered on the extensive lowland plains of east central China. As the Yangtze exits from the last gorge, it enters a complex system of lakes, marshes, and multiple river channels developed on the plains of Hunan and Hubei Provinces. Because this vast region's elevation is less than one hundred feet, it serves as a natural flood regulation basin. The hundreds of lakes scattered throughout, including Lake Dongting, the second-largest lake in China, help minimize damaging floods by absorbing some flood waters. Because of this region's ability to absorb floodwaters, levels fluctuate considerably between the flood and low-flow seasons. This is also the reach where three main tributaries, the Yuan, Xiang, and Han, and many smaller ones join the Yangtze.

The middle reach that is fed by the Yangtze and its many tributaries contains the majority of the Yangtze basin's crop production and population. This stretch of river basin is famed as one of the world's most abundant croplands due entirely to the extensive tracts of highly nutritious silt deposited here each year by the Yangtze. During the rainy season, when the river often overflows its banks, the floodwaters deposit a thick layer of silt carried down from the mountainous regions in the upper reach.

Lower Reach: The Land of Fish and Rice

The lower reach, from the city of Hukou to the sea, is another six hundred miles. Most of this segment is very close to sea level, creating an enormous lakelike environment. Because of this watery morass, the lower reach is said to be an ideal habitat where both fish and rice can flourish.

When the Yangtze reaches the city of Zhenjiang, about two hundred miles inland from its mouth, the river is virtually at sea level. This last two-hundred-mile stretch is also called the Yangtze Delta because the river fans out to form a delta or triangular-shaped estuary more than one hundred miles wide.

The Yangtze Delta consists of a large number of branches, tributaries, lakes, ancient riverbeds, and marshes that are

The Legend of the Three Gorges

The majesty and grandeur of the dozens of peaks rising high above the Three Gorges stretch of the Yangtze have been celebrated throughout the entire country for thousands of years. A site of such natural beauty and serenity naturally became a source for fanciful stories describing its origin.

The legend surrounding the creation of the Three Gorges provides a creative visual drama that can be matched only by the gorges themselves. Ancient traditional stories relate that back in the mists of time, when the planet was still new, an assortment of gods was maneuvering for power over the kingdom of China. At that primeval time, the great Yu-wang seized control of the rivers. He then ascended to the top of Tu-san Mountain where he meditated for centuries on the best way to design a river that would run from heaven to earth. When he was done, he carved all the rivers on the back of a tortoise shell and ordered that the river to heaven run eastward, through the mountains to the sea. But the obstinate spirits that controlled the mountains refused to agree. Yu-wang then appealed to the wizard Wu-tze and she agreed to help him. Then, with a mighty blow from her nostrils, she blasted a colossal canyon halfway through the reluctant mountains. The effort exhausted her before she could complete the entire route, so she retired to a cave where she lives to this very day. Yu-wang himself discovered a magical ax with which he hacked out the Three Gorges and unleashed the roaring torrents that now coil and hiss like dragons through the mountains of southern China. Thus began the legend of the Three Great Gorges.

A farmer in the Yunnan province carries a harvest of rice near the Yangtze's lower reach.

connected with the main channel. Lake Tai is notable as the largest lake in the delta. The width of the Yangtze at the beginning of the delta ranges from about three-quarters of a mile to almost a mile and a half. Further downriver, however, the channel gradually widens and becomes a large estuary, the width of which exceeds fifty miles near the mouth of the river.

Limnologists, scientists who specialize in the study of freshwater systems, and hydrologists estimate the daily river discharge to be about 2 billion cubic yards. Associated with this discharge is a heavy load of silt. The magnitude of this load is best revealed in satellite photographs of the region that depict an enormous brown plume extending miles out to sea. It is estimated that more than 150 million cubic yards of sediment accumulate here every year. The combination of rich sediments, a hot wet summer, and a shallow water table leads to bountiful rice crops. Rice is by far the most important summer crop but the delta also sustains cotton, soybeans, and some corn.

Why the Yangtze River flows out of the Kunlun Mountains on the Qinghai-Tibet plateau and plummets through more than two thousand miles of mountainous gorges before slowing and widening near the East China Sea is explained by geologic activity millions of years ago.

Geology of the Yangtze

The immense Tibetan mountain range began to form between 40 and 50 million years ago when the drifting Indian landmass to the south collided with the more stationary Eurasian landmasses. Geologists Peter Molnar and Paul Tapponier point out that this collision is still taking place at the rate of about five centimeters a year which accounts for the fact that the tallest peaks continue to gain height.

The pressure caused by this grand collision thrust the land skyward, called an "upwarp" by geologists, forming the jagged Tibetan peaks. Prior to the upwarp, this region was submerged beneath the ocean. But following the upwarp and the eventual flow of streams and rivers, the mountains began to erode and the rivers began to deposit thousands of feet of silt that gradually displaced the seawater. Molnar and Tapponier continue to explain that the pressure has had the effect of forcing the Yangtze east, much "Like toothpaste squeezed from a tube."[3]

A secondary effect of the upwarp was the formation of the great Cathaysian geosyncline, a trough cut through rocks that the Yangtze and many of its tributaries follow for more than a thousand miles. The upwarp and this geosyncline have combined to create an enormous landmass that is far more mountainous than flat. Compared to the United States, for example, where 30 percent of the land is flat and arable, in China it is only 11 percent.

Amazing Animals Along the Yangtze

The Yangtze River basin is home to a remarkable array of animal life. There are more than 3,400 species of vertebrates, nearly 400 mammal species, 1,000 species of birds, more than 300 species of reptiles, and 200 species of amphibians. Of this collection, more than 100 species are indigenous to the river basin including the giant panda, golden-haired monkey, South China tiger, brown-eared pheasant, white-flag dolphin, Chinese alligator, and red-crowned crane.

The towering peaks and secluded valleys of the Tibetan plateau are rich with some of the world's most diverse and rarest high-elevation animals. Of particular interest to zoologists are the occasional snow leopards, red pandas, and lynx that come to the river to drink and feed. Of interest to hearty nomadic tribes for food and work are the Tibetan yak, Tibetan antelope, geese, and wild long-haired donkeys.

A Yangtze River alligator preys on a helpless chick. The alligator is just one of many animal species to make its home in the Yangtze River basin.

A wild panda visits the home of her Sichuan neighbors to enjoy a few fresh bamboo shoots.

Living high in the forests within the middle reach is an equally exquisite collection of mammals and birds. Many species of squirrel, and monkeys including the golden and snub-nosed, live here as well as the giant panda, clouded leopard, the gaur (a species of wild ox), sun bear, golden swallow, and white pheasant.

Two of the most notable and interesting animals that dwell in the river are the baiji dolphin and the finless porpoise. Known as "panda in water," the baiji dolphin is a living fossil. Paleontologists believe that its ancestors moved from land to water over 70 million years ago. This dolphin has a stocky body and a long, thin snout, which is not quite flat and tilts up slightly. Small eyes are near the top of its head, and tiny ear openings are located where most dolphins have eyes. The baiji's coloring is a pale smoked gray with white on the stomach. It catches and chews its prey with thirty to thirty-five coned-shaped teeth on each jaw.

Among the smallest creatures in the marine mammal family is the finless porpoise. At an average length of five feet, this pale gray-blue porpoise has a small mouth that curves slightly upwards and a slight depression behind the blowhole. Finless porpoises prefer to live in shallow warm waters like those of the lower Yangtze. They are easily identifiable by their lack of dorsal fins. Instead of a fin, they have a ridge covered in circular wartlike tubercles or bumps along their backs that runs from above the flippers to the beginning of their tails.

Plant Life

The Yangtze River basin is home to an abundance of plant life. Estimates exceed fifteen thousand species of higher-order plants. In addition, there are more than five thousand species of woody plants, including two thousand tree species. Of all the plant life, fifteen hundred species are edible and two thousand are used in various forms of medicine. The better-known Chinese herbal medicines from the Yangtze basin are ginseng, Changbai safflower, and Chinese wolfberry.

Plant life varies throughout the many climatic regions of the Yangtze basin. High in the Tibetan plateau, well above the timberline, only a variety of short grasses and low-lying simple flowering plants are evident. Although plant life is sparse, the intense sun in the thin atmosphere brings out some of the most vivid colors found anywhere along the river.

The lower elevation forests provide a nutrient-rich habitat for a number of food trees including almond, walnut, citrus, cherry, longan, and litchi. Botanists believe that the litchi may have first come into cultivation in this area. Numerous mountain ranges also support many of the conifer and magnolia families. At lower mountain elevations, large stands of trees flourish. Forests along stretches of the Yangtze produce groves of several species of the oak family and many varieties of pine, various laurels, and aromatic cedars.

Yet of all the species of plants, the one most revered is the bamboo, which belongs to the grass family. It is distinguished by the special structure of its stem, or "culm," and its plentiful but thin leaves. Bamboo's most striking characteristic is its immense vitality. One species of bamboo has been known to grow over four feet in twenty-four hours. Others can reach maturity—more than twenty feet tall—within sixty days and live for more than one hundred years.

Bamboo is also regarded as the most versatile of all flora along the Yangtze. It is cut and used for construction of boats, houses, scaffolding, carts, floors, and even bridges. It is also used to make a variety of tools for farming, channeling water, digging, and serving food. Its long fibers can be stripped and woven into ropes, fishing line, hammocks,

Factory workers carry bundles of bamboo into a paper manufacturing plant. Bamboo is put to many uses in China.

sleeping mats, sandals, and a seemingly endless variety of other common applications.

This rich and varied collection of flora thrives on a plentiful supply of water during the summer rains. The remainder of the year, although light rains can be anticipated, these plants depend on their deep root systems to locate water. Were it not for summer floods, however, few of the species could survive.

The Floods of Summer

The floods of summer are an annual climatic phenomenon along the Yangtze. When the late spring and early summer sun begins to warm the winter snow pack and glacial for-

Homes along the banks of the Yangtze River are flooded during the summer months. Flooding along the river is an annual occurrence.

mations, the upper 75 percent of the river's course begins to swell as the melt cascades down dozens of small streams through the upper reach of the Yangtze. The amount of melted water that will rush forward down the river is unpredictable. Some years, when the winter snows are light or when the summer temperatures are lower than average, the Yangtze fails to reach its maximum capacity. But other years, just the opposite combination of climatic conditions can cause severe flooding.

At this same time of year, a second annual climatic phenomenon occurs—the Chinese monsoon season arrives over the Asian continent. The annual monsoon results from the contrast between the temperatures over the land and ocean. During the summer months as the land heats up, monsoon winds blow from the southwest bringing hot winds and heavy rains throughout the southern Yangtze basin. Later, during the winter, the winds blow from the northeast bringing drought conditions.

When snowmelt meets monsoon rains, the Yangtze rises. Flooding along the middle and especially the lower reaches is both common and anticipated. Average monsoon rainfall of forty-two inches over the six-month monsoon season can cause the narrow gorges of the upper reach to rise rapidly—as much as thirty feet in a single day. This sort of flooding, which can be destructive within the gorges, is a valuable and welcomed resource to farmers on the broad plains of the lower reach. They welcome the normal saturation of their land with water and tons of nutritious silt.

When both snowmelt and rains are unusually heavy, however, the combination can be fatal. Fierce, torrential downpours dropping several inches in a single day, or two feet within one week can inflict catastrophic damage along the entire length of the Yangtze. In the mountainous regions of much of the upper reach, where the river is hemmed in by steep mountains, the river has been known to rise 130 feet above the normal elevation. Entire communities located in the passes have been swept downriver. When such a wall of water eventually reaches the broad plains of the middle and lower reaches, the pressure immediately fans out and sends choppy surges of water as far as one hundred miles in either direction, inundating both large and small communities.

Fortunately for the Yangtze farmers and fishermen, such catastrophic floods are rare occurrences. Most years the Yangtze behaves predictably, providing villagers and city dwellers with most of their basic needs. Although the river is occasionally feared, the Yangtze has been China's most important lifeline since the beginning of Chinese civilization thousands of years ago.

2

．．．．．．．．．．

China's Lifeline

Great rivers have always been the primal source of early civilizations. Like the Nile in Egypt, the Ganges in India, and the Tigris and Euphrates in ancient Mesopotamia, the Yangtze was the cradle of early civilization in China. Thousands of years ago, this magnificent river served to irrigate crops, provide fish, transport commerce, and define the ancient Chinese culture. Chinese historians recognize three ancient cultures along the Yangtze, each of which occupied a different stretch of the river as far back as 3000 B.C. Chinese scholar Elizabeth Childs-Johnson sums up the significance of the Yangtze to these early cultures:

> The Yangtze is revered for its role in providing sustenance to those who inhabit its banks. For thousands of years, these people have tilled its fertile plains, fished its deep pools and navigated its channels, reaping its benefits as a conduit of trade. It is no wonder the river is considered "China's Lifeline."[4]

Excavations of burial sites have revealed great stories about the lives of early Yangtze civilizations. Archaeologists entering several burial mounds on the banks of the lower

Yangtze River uncovered stone and ceramic tools used for farming, hunting, and fishing. These tools included the axe, plowshare, adze, chisel, sickle, the spearhead, arrow point, and fishhook. Reviewing the hoard of archaeological evidence, professor Kwang-Chih Chang of Yale University, concluded, "The inhabitants of the villages were farmers, hunters, fishers, and collectors."[5]

Agriculture

There is an old saying in China that food is the god of the people. To fulfill this basic requirement, agriculture plays an important part within all three reaches of the Yangtze basin. Beginning with the earliest settlements, the river has always been the central artery of China's breadbasket. Agriculture was made possible and highly bountiful in the river's middle and lower reaches by the combination of annual flooding and the warm humid climate. Archaeologists' findings of piles of carbonized rice in ancient burial mounds attest to the importance of this crop thriving in the wet lower Yangtze environment.

Rice was an ideal crop for the lower Yangtze. Farmers living in primitive villages close to the flat delta understood the value of the river's natural flooding to the growth of rice. Rice thrives in warm climates where fields are constantly saturated by water and silt. This combination of climate and geography plus the added bonus of the highly nutritional silt made rice the most important crop along the Yangtze. Based on excavations, archaeologists estimate that rice accounted for between 80 and 90 percent of grains eaten by the ancient Chinese.

Evidence from archaeologists indicates that more than rice was grown. Professor Robert Temple, in his book, *The Genius of China: 3,000 Years of Science, Discovery, and Invention*, reports the discovery of the plowshare, called the *kuan*, which was only needed to break up dry soil that would have existed further from the water-soaked rice fields. Temple further indicates the findings of carbonized grains other than rice, primarily wheat and oats. These find-

ings indicate that farming took place many miles from the river where lighter flooding occurred or where primitive forms of irrigation have been used. Remnants of cotton fibers from clothing are also clear evidence of local cotton production.

Rice fields in the Sichuan Province are irrigated with water from the Yangtze River. Rice is historically the most important crop grown along the river.

Whatever crops were planted, farmers had to take their chances with the monsoon rains. Without being able to predict the strength of the rains, they often mitigated their risks by planting in more than just one field. Farmers were known to plant some rice fields close to the river and other grains farther away. By employing the technique of farming multiple small plots instead of one large plot, they hoped to avoid complete devastation in the event the monsoon rains were excessively heavy or excessively light. Professor Chang believes that the average farmer worked a total of three to seven acres and he adds, "This area had the environment potential to provide for an affluent society in prehistoric times as well as in the present."[6]

Aquaculture

Aquaculture, as a way of controlling and harvesting fish and water plants, dates back to 2000 B.C. along the lower Yangtze. In the Yangtze Delta, where water could be counted on year-round, the early villagers planted certain fruit-bearing plants heavily dependent upon nutritious water and harvested them like rice. The advantage of controlling the planting of certain fruit-bearing aquatic plants, according to professor Chang, was that farmers could plant them densely and then protect them from scavenging land animals and birds. Chang studied excavations, writings, and the art of early Yangtze River cultures and concluded:

> The freshwater vegetation was a huge advantage for the inhabitants and they exploited and cultivated [these plants] for their benefit. Aquaculture has been practiced here since the Neolithic times. The products of such are water-caltrops [vines], flax nuts, lotus seeds and roots, water chestnuts, wild rice, and many others. Although these plants occur in countries and continents beyond China, they are not cultivated anywhere but in China. This makes such a discovery as this very unique and important not only to China, but to the study of agriculture.[7]

Josh Goldman, president of Fins Technology, a company specializing in aquaculture for fish farming, confirms that the Chinese practiced aquaculture to raise fish as well as edible plants. He recounts that, "The Chinese developed techniques for raising fish for consumption and for ornamental purposes. In 475 BC, Fan Lai, a fish farmer and writer, produced his well-known Chinese treatise on carp culture."[8] In his book, Fan Lai recommends the best procedures for breeding and raising fish for commercial consumption. The existence of this book suggests to historians that fish farming was widespread during this very early period.

Fish farming took place in the flooded rice fields. Rice fields were preferred because farmers knew that the fish could survive on the rice kernels that fell into the water along with insect larva and other small bits of food washed in by the river's flow. Fish farmers learned that by enclosing fish in rice fields with bamboo fences or reed mats, the fish would not be able to escape and predators would not be able to enter. In this very primitive form of fish farming, the fish grew without much labor demanded of the farmer, and when they reached maturity they were easily speared or scooped up in nets. To protect the fish in the event the water level fell dangerously low, farmers dug deep furrows in the fields to provide a place where the fish could survive.

Fishing

The size and volume of the Yangtze was too treacherous for ancient fishermen. Rather than venture out into the middle of the river to find fish, early peoples searched the smaller tributaries and tranquil side canyons, where many species of fish found refuge for feeding and spawning. Catching the fish was done in one of several ways that included hooks and lines, nets, and spears.

Archaeologists speculate that most early fishermen fished with hook and line. Fishhooks are the most commonly found fishing tools in the excavations of villages along the Yangtze. Made of bone, ceramics, antler, and even stone, the fishhooks indicate the ancient Chinese had a significant dependence upon fish for their diets. Stories in early Chinese literature indicate that early fishermen learned to attach bells to their lines which rang as soon as a fish swallowed the hook. The use of the bell allowed one fisherman to drop multiple lines in the water simultaneously yet land each fish as soon as it took a hook.

One of the most interesting ancient tools for fishing found in excavations was the long-handled Chinese trident

Chinese fishermen along the Yangtze River use modern replicas of the ancient wushu *tool to spear their catch.*

called the *wushu*, meaning fork in Chinese. With two prongs on the head it is called the horn fork; with three prongs, the trident or three-pronged fork. The handle was twelve to thirteen feet long and weighed about five pounds. These primitive fish-catching forks that have been unearthed in the ruins of several provinces have a joint at the end of the handle for fixing a rope. When the fork was thrown, it could be recovered by pulling on the attached rope.

Ancient paintings indicate that fishermen sometimes used nets, working in groups in shallow streams. They stretched a net made of the long fibers of bamboo across a stream and secured it to trees on either bank. They then waded downstream two to three hundred yards and banged bamboo poles up and down to frighten the fish toward the net. When both the fish and the men were close to the net, two of the fishermen jumped from the water, untied the net from the trees, and enclosed it around the fish that had been herded into it.

Anthropologists believe that fish was the major source of protein eaten by those along the Yangtze but early Chinese also enjoyed and depended upon red meat and fowl to vary their diets. Primitive societies were just as adept at hunting along the river as they were at fishing in it.

Hunting

Hunting provided ancient Chinese along the Yangtze with a significant supply of their protein as a welcome alternative to fish. According to professor Chang, "Although the [ancient] Shu people had domestic animals [to eat] they also hunted wild game such as boar, elephant and deer. These animals were extremely important to the civilization."[9]

Numerous spear points and arrowheads excavated by archaeologists suggest that they were the weapons of choice for hunting game the size of wild boar and deer. Typically hunters awaited their game in a secluded spot, often a drinking pool at the river's edge. Hiding in brush or overhanging limbs, the hunter waited with a bow and arrows until the game was distracted while drinking.

Larger kills, such as elephant and rhinoceros, were a very different matter. As evidenced by ancient drawings depicting the hunt, two techniques for large game were used: an attack of many hunters who descended upon a slow-moving, large animal in unison, driving their spears into its belly; and the use of kill pits.

Kill pits were deep holes in the ground large enough to engulf an animal the size of an elephant. The opening was concealed with a thin layer of limbs, leaves, and dirt. Hunters then singled out one animal from a herd and chased it toward the disguised pit. As soon as the heavy animal ran across the thin covering, the animal crashed through the branches and was trapped. At that point, spear throwers and archers moved in for the kill.

Trained packs of large dogs were also effectively employed in the hunt. The earliest mention of Tibetan mastiffs used in the Yangtze basin for hunting bear and wolves comes from 1121 B.C., when it was written that the emperor of China received such a dog as a gift.

Travel on the Yangtze

The river has always been the main artery of water transportation between eastern and western China. The cruising range of its trunk river and hundreds of tributaries makes up 70 percent of China's total inland navigation, and its water transport capacity accounts for 80 percent of the total inland water transport capacity. In 1290, Marco Polo, the first Westerner to visit the Yangtze from his native city of Venice, Italy, wrote:

> A great number of cities and large towns are situated on its banks, and more than two hundred, with sixteen provinces, partake of the advantages of its navigation, by which the transport of merchandise is carried on to an extent that might appear incredible to those who have not had an opportunity of witnessing it.[10]

The early boats on the Yangtze were an expression of the culture; people traveled on them, worked on them, and even lived on them. Archaeological evidence of ancient boats indicate that most were canoe-shaped wooden boats often large enough for only three or four passengers. On occasion a larger boat might seat ten people or accommodate as much as two tons of cargo. These canoes were made of planks lashed together with leather strips and sealed with resin. Propulsion for most of these boats was a single *yuloh*, a long wood sculling oar that extended into the water from the boat's stern and was pushed from side to side to drive the boat.

Later in history, sometime around the twelfth century A.D., larger, more sophisticated boats were needed to navigate the Yangtze. The three distinct designs that evolved along the river were *sanpans* (also spelled sampans), mean-

ing three planks wide; the larger *wupans*, meaning five planks wide; and the largest of the river boats, junks. Whichever boat was used, travelers were at the mercy of the river's currents because none of these boats moved quickly against it. A simple trip that might take six to eight days downriver might take thirty days against the current and even forty during the flood season. It was during the flood season that the river raced so violently that the boats had to be pulled from the water for many days and sometimes dragged across land to a safer spot upriver. Death from boats being swept away or smashed against protruding boulders was a risk that all who dared to ply the river during a high flood accepted.

Both the *sanpan* and *wupan* are very similar in design, the only difference being size. Neither boat has sails. The

Fishermen steady a wupan *boat to cross a steep wake. Local craftsmen have built these sturdy boats for nearly a millennium.*

Junk Trackers

Chinese junks had little success moving upriver against the current. Their fixed sails prevented tacking maneuvers that normally allow ships to sail against the wind or against a strong current. For this reason, moving the junks upstream required many dozens of men, called trackers, to pull the junks with long ropes tied to chest harnesses. Once young boys entered one of the gangs of trackers, he never knew any other type of employment.

Barefooted trackers moved in unison along muddy paths and sloping hillsides leaning against their rope harnesses. As they struggled against the resistance of the junk in the water, each tracker leaned forward until his torso was bent parallel to the mud and his fingers dug into the mud providing extra traction. Since paths were narrow and hillsides irregular,

the teams of tethered men fanned out forming what appeared at a distance to be a great web of ropes pulling the junk. Maintaining momentum was demanded by the tracking bosses who rhythmically chanted songs to keep the men moving at precisely the same pace.

Under no circumstances did the bosses allow the web of straining men to stop. A crew of one hundred trackers that lost momentum and ground to a halt might not be able to get started again. Even worse, the whole crew might be dragged down the mountain slope into the river if the junk were swept away by the current. They knew that trackers who slipped would have to be cut loose, sometimes to fall to certain death, rather than take the whole line of coolies down with them.

Chinese junks (pictured) have difficulty moving upstream, and require a crew to pull the ships along.

smaller of the two is barely eighteen feet overall, with a beam of five feet and depth of two. This boat was a favorite for families to live on and for light freight hauling. The *wupan* measures twenty-three feet long on average and could accommodate a family and a fair amount of freight. In the center of these boats would be a section of overhead bamboo and mats to provide modest shelter from the sun and tropical rains. Near the stern would be a small cook-stove where the rower could keep an eye on the meal that was cooking while he rowed.

Both the *sanpan* and *wupan* were propelled only by currents, winds, and a single *yuloh*. The flat section of the *yuloh* extends under the water. Its cylinder-shaped handle, about four inches in diameter, is held in place by a wooden yoke. Propulsion is achieved when a standing rower pushes the handle back and forth moving the boat along at two or three miles per hour.

The junk was the workhorse of the river. It is a large, flat-bottomed, high-sterned vessel with a square bow and stern. It typically had three masts that stood at different angles; the tallest stands just front of center, the second tallest occupies the bow and the smallest is on the stern. The sails are mere squares of rough cloth fastened to stout spars at either end and stiffened with bamboo poles that resembled ribs. It is large enough to function as a houseboat, traveling hotel, a floating restaurant, and was commonly used as the freighter of the Yangtze.

Canals

Early Yangtze civilizations recognized the significance of the river for transportation but also understood its shortcomings. Small wooden boats caught in an occasional sudden flash flood or in rough white-water currents were often smashed, dumping crews and cargo into the treacherous waters. Early peoples also realized that not all cities had access to the Yangtze or one of its hundreds of tributaries. For them, transportation was an arduous job that took place along roads that made for slow shipping of cargo on the backs of porters and donkeys.

To solve these two problems, city planners as far back as the eighth century B.C. conceived the idea of digging canals to connect cities and to connect rivers. Short distances less than ten miles could not justify the expense of digging even small canals fifteen feet wide and four feet deep across flat land. Longer distances, however, especially between two large inland cities, made construction cost effective. Using human and animal power, a network of canals was constructed primarily for the transportation of grains grown in wet lowland areas to cities in drier climates farther from the water.

The largest single canal network, built during most of the third century B.C., linked an inland area of two thousand square miles. Called the *Tu-chiang Yen*, meaning the All River Canal, this enterprise not only provided for travel but also irrigation. It carried water from the Yangtze and, according to Chinese historian Joseph Needham, this network, "Supported a population of about five million people . . . and freed them from the dangers of drought and floods. It can be compared only with the ancient works [canals] of the Nile."[11]

Over time canals became longer and more complex to construct. Changes in elevation required primitive locks to raise and lower boats, and in some cases larger boats had to first be dragged out of one canal by men pulling on ropes, then transferred to another canal. This tricky engineering required the use of an inclined plane faced with stone. The stone created less friction than dirt banks against the bottom of the boats as they were pulled from the water. Use of inclined planes was limited, however, because long boats tended to crack in half if not properly supported when released from the plane.

As a large network of canals evolved throughout the middle and lower reaches, the largest canal ever, the Grand Canal of China, was constructed. The building of this Herculean canal began in 486 B.C. at the Yangtze port city

River barges contend with gridlock conditions along the Grand Canal, the largest manmade waterway in the world.

of Hangzhou. In A.D. 610 the canal, now 1,114 miles long with twenty-four locks and sixty bridges, reached Beijing.

The ancient Chinese believed rivers, canals, and boats were important even in the afterlife. So central to life was the Yangtze that when people died, they still wanted to remain close by. Early river cultures incorporated the river and boats into their funeral rituals that have only recently been brought to light by archaeologists digging in the upper and middle reaches.

The Grand Canal

The Grand Canal is the world's longest man-made waterway. Extending nearly twelve hundred miles from Hangzhou on the Yangtze all the way north to the city Beijing, this canal is China's only major north-south waterway. In its time, it provided safer transport of passengers and cargo than could be found by risking storms and pirates on the open seas.

The Grand Canal of Imperial China was a massive public works project that, in its final form, connected the political center of the empire in the north with the economic and agricultural center in the south along the Yangtze River. The creation of an imperial canal system during the Sui-Tang period marked the culmination of centuries of water control projects and facilitated the expansion and control of an increasingly large empire. The expansion of the canal system and the communications it provided helped solidify China's expansive empire. At its height, an estimated four hundred thousand tons of grain in addition to mountains of other nonedible commerce were shipped from the Yangtze north to the capital each year on the canal.

The canal was an impressive engineering accomplishment. Estimates suggest that the project occupied five million workers, half of whom died on the job from disease, malnutrition, or starvation. Depths of the canal ranged between seven and eleven feet and could be regulated by a series of seventy-five sluices, gates made from wood planks, that could be fully or partially closed. To accommodate travel in both directions simultaneously, the canal was dug between fifty and one hundred feet wide. The banks were protected by stone in many places, and stone bridges were built across the canal. The boats were moved along the canal mainly by sail but oars were employed in the event of adverse winds or no wind at all. Smaller boats were pulled by gangs of men.

River Burials

The Yangtze played a key role in ancient death rituals. Archaeologists have uncovered a variety of funeral styles along the Yangtze riverbanks that include earth mounds, evidence of water burials, open exposure graves, and the two most interesting and unusual of them all, suspended coffins and boat burials.

Many ancient coffins have been found hanging halfway up a mountain cliff in the Three Gorges. People put the bodies of the deceased into wooden coffins, which were then placed in caves along the walls of gorges high above the waterline. These suspended coffins were a unique funeral style for the ancient Ba people, who mainly inhabited the Three Gorges region. These suspended coffins are said to date back to the Ming dynasty, between A.D. 1368 and 1644 but no one is sure how or why this custom came about.

Taking the form of a ship, most coffins were carved out of one whole piece of wood. According to local people, the location of the coffins was determined by the social prestige of the deceased. The more honorable the deceased were, the higher the coffins were placed. It was believed that hanging the coffins in this manner prevented bodies from being taken by wild animals and that the souls of the deceased would be blessed and released to the river.

The other means by which ancient Chinese demonstrated their respect for the river was the use of burial boats. Cemeteries excavated along the riverbed revealed individual graves perpendicular to the river bank. Within them were found long narrow flat-bottom canoes with two beveled ends and an opening at the top. Inside these canoe coffins were bronze artifacts: axes, spears, arrowheads, vessels, belts, hooks, knives, and stamps used as sealing stamps on letters. According to historian Carolyn Walker and colleagues, the boat burials occurred because

> [boats] were important transportation tools, and so the boat became an important symbol. People would need a boat to survive in another world. Some scholars have further suggested that the Ba might have thought their souls would be taken back to their ancestral lands in these boats.[12]

These simple burial rites speak volumes about the respect and appreciation that early cultures held for the Yangtze. The river was home for many families, for some it was the provider of a lifetime of food, and still for others their place of work, recreation, and companionship with fellow river dwellers. Although anthropologists and archaeologists believe this simplicity of life existed for about nine thousand years, such a poetic agrarian relationship was not destined to last forever.

3
· · · · · · · · ·

Taming and
Developing the Dragon

For thousands of years Yangtze rice farmers, fishermen, craftsmen, and merchants survived on the bounty of the river without the need to alter the ways of this great lifeline. The natural rhythm of the river provided them a simple yet fairly steady and predictable tempo that sustained tens of millions from birth to death. To the early cultures of the Yangtze, the river was to be revered and even worshiped but never questioned or altered to suit their transitory needs.

As constant as the river's flow was the constancy of the Chinese people as well. Their rural agrarian economy continued well into the twentieth century, since China was isolated on all sides by imposing natural barriers against foreign invasion and outside influence. Although nineteenth century European and American industrial giants occasionally made brief incursions up the Yangtze to evaluate its potential for industrial production and commercial exploitation, none was welcomed by the Chinese and none stayed long. All attempts to awaken the "Sleeping Dragon" by conquering the river with steamboats and opening it to industry and foreign trade failed to take root until the twentieth century.

In October 1949 the challenging yet relatively placid life along the Yangtze came to an abrupt end—not from outside foreign intervention—but rather from within. Following a violent social revolution in China, Mao Zedong (Tze-tung), the chairman of the Chinese Communist Party, proclaimed the establishment of the incipient People's Republic of China. At the forefront of the agenda was the decision to improve the nation's economy by quickly industrializing the country while continuing to support the well-established agrarian economy. Mao hoped to improve the lives of all Chinese by achieving higher living standards, better education, and improved medical care. Such an ambitious undertaking was greatly dependent upon the waters of the Yangtze.

Chinese Communist leader Mao Zedong (pictured on poster) relied heavily on the Yangtze River in his plans for the country's industrial and economic development.

The Great Leap Forward: Factories on the Yangtze

A combination of internal and external factors bogged down any industrial momentum gained by the revolution, but finally in 1958 Mao launched the Great Leap Forward campaign. The Great Leap Forward aimed at accomplishing the economic and industrial development of the country at a vastly faster pace and with better results than had taken place before. Its emphasis on rapid industrialization meant gearing up production of all natural resources that were needed to fuel factories. Particular emphasis was placed on the mining of coal and chemicals, clear-cutting the forests, the production of steel and petroleum, manufacturing paper products, and the generation of electricity.

The Yangtze was destined to play a major role in these endeavors. As the largest river in China with the most extensive network of tributaries, it reached more than one third of China's population and nurtured half of the nation's food production. It also flowed through the heart of China's densest forests and mines, all of which would be tapped to drive the factories of the new economy. Mao Zedong and his ministers also understood the value of the Yangtze as the highway that would move natural resources to factories built along the river's banks and then carry the finished products to foreign markets throughout much of China and the world. But Mao also understood that before he could exploit the dragon, he would first need to tame and develop it.

Mao recognized that achieving these goals on the Yangtze would require different solutions from one reach along the river to the next. He also recognized that common to all economic goals would be the need for flood control, hydroelectric generation, and improved industrial and agricultural water distribution. Most of all, Mao recognized that meeting all of these objectives would require the damming of the river.

Ancient Plank Roads

In ancient times nearly all transportation in the Three Gorges region was dependent on boats plying the waterway. Hikers chanced narrow dirt and mud trails close to the water but when floods raced through the gorges, the trails were washed away and foot travel came to a halt. To remedy this annual interruption for foot travelers, someone conceived the idea of building a wood plank road high enough above the water to allow hikers to walk the gorges any time of year. The existence of this plank road is still discernible at the mouth of the Thatched Cottage River where holes bored in the stone to support the planks can still be seen.

About 300 B.C., those who engineered this road began by drilling holes into the rock wall on one side of the Yangtze about forty feet above the normal elevation of the river.

These holes were drilled level and about six feet apart along about forty miles of the river. A hefty wood post, about six-by-six inches thick, was then rammed into each hole, protruding out from the wall about twelve feet. On top of this line of posts and perpendicular to them were nailed long planks that served as the footpath.

Literary references from the time when the plank road was in use make references to a chain rail along the outside of the road to prevent hikers from unfortunate falls. They also record that the road was wide enough for travel in both directions simultaneously or for one sedan (covered chair) carried by eight men. Nowadays, all of the wood posts and planks are gone. Nonetheless, the holes running down the side of the cliff are still visible.

Damming the Yangtze

The mighty Yangtze was known to have two personae: one the benign provider of rich soil for the cultivation of food and clear clean water for bountiful catches of fish and the other the destroyer of fields and villages when it flooded. A poem of unknown origin quoted in Lyman P. van Slyke's book, *Yangtze: Nature, History and the River* expresses the anguish and sorrow caused by occasional Yangtze floods:

Pitiful people—victims of flood.

Temples awash, ancestral graves submerged,

Houses like fish in a stewpot.

Good fortune brings dense green shoots,

Then all at once the fields become white waves.

Aiya, [an expression of dismay] why is the river god
    so ruthless?

Though you raise your head and cry unto heaven,

Heaven answers not.[13]

Mao knew that the Yangtze could be ferocious. Every twenty years or so, during an abnormally wet monsoon season, an avalanche of water washed down the gorges of the middle reach sweeping away towns, villages, boats, and everyone unfortunate enough to be caught in its path. Once the wall of water entered the broad delta region closer to the ocean it fanned out for miles, swallowing everything in its path.

During the 1950s Chinese engineers concluded that controlling the occasional catastrophic flooding of the Yangtze required a series of strategically placed dams. Before that time, only twenty-three large- and medium-scale dams and reservoirs existed in all of China but none were in the Yangtze River basin. Dams on the Yangtze and its tributaries were to act as catchments as well as diversions. At catchment and storage dams, during periods of flooding the water is stored in reservoirs and later safely released during periods of drought. At diversion dams, floodwaters are trapped and diverted to drier regions in need of water.

The first great dam on the Yangtze was built between 1958 and 1974 at the city of Danjiangkou on the Han River at its confluence with the Yangtze. This diversion dam, constructed of earth and rock and enclosed within a steel and concrete outer casing, annually reroutes an average of 18 billion cubic yards of water to parched northern provinces where it is desperately needed. At the same time it reduces

The Yangtze town of Wushan (pictured) will be completely submerged after the massive Three Gorges Dam project is finished.

the possibility for flooding of the lower reach of the Yangtze River. Following the success of this diversion dam, hundreds more quickly dotted other tributaries of the Yangtze.

Soon factories came to life on the river, and the traditional agricultural economy gave way to industry. The first sign of the new economy was a sudden spike in the demand for electricity. Prior to this time, most electricity was generated by burning coal, which caused severe air pollution in the form of concentrations of nitrogen oxide, hydrocarbons, and carbon monoxide. To increase electricity production and reduce air pollution, engineers aggressively moved forward with the construction of hydroelectric generators on all new dams.

Between 1970 and 1988, Chinese engineers constructed the Gezhouba Dam on the Yangtze near the city of I-ch'ang in one of the narrows in the middle reach. The concrete dam is 8,500 feet long and 175 feet tall. Although the storage capacity is only 3 billion cubic yards of water, significantly less than the Yangtze's first great dam, it annually generates 5.7 billion kilowatts of electricity with its twenty-one generators. This load of electricity is shared among several major cities badly in need of it such as Wuhan and Shanghai as well as villages in the provinces of Henan to the north and Hunan to the south.

These two large dams paid immediate dividends to the people of China. They have been so successful in reducing flood conditions, diverting excess water to drier cities and fields, and generating pollution-free electricity that hundreds more were subsequently added. With the assistance of the Yangtze dams, agriculture and factory production briskly increased to the delight of Mao and all living along the ancient waterway.

Three Gorges Dam

Most of the hundreds of dams were relatively small by modern standards and were built on tributaries of the Yangtze. As a consequence, occasional floods continued to sweep down the gorges of the middle and lower reaches of the river on their dash to the sea, destroying villages and farmland that lay in their path. For nearly one hundred years, the one spot on the Yangtze that appeared best suited for a major dam was the Three Gorges near the city of Fengjie. In 1994 construction began on the Three Gorges Dam, which is scheduled for completion in 2009.

The father of modern China, Sun Yat-sen, is credited with being the first to propose a hydroelectric dam at Three Gorges in 1919. And in 1954, after devastating floods along the Yangtze that killed thousands, Mao Zedong ordered feasibility studies on damming the river. In 1992 the People's Republic of China approved the project of damming the river with a massive wall of concrete

Construction cranes work on the Three Gorges Dam project. When completed, it will be the world's largest dam and hydroelectric power plant.

and steel—a fifteen-year project that, when completed, will create the world's largest dam and hydroelectric power plant.

The country's largest construction project ever undertaken, the gargantuan dam will be nearly a mile and a half across and six hundred feet high, holding back a reservoir four hundred miles long. This concrete and steel monolith will control downriver flooding that has plagued China for millennia and will contain the world's biggest hydropower plant to help fuel the nation's economic boom into the next century.

Chinese authorities hope the dam will take care of several major national problems with a single monumental stroke. The Three Gorges project is seen as an important future source of energy for China's growing electrical consumption. It is also expected to tame the river's occasional flood downriver. The Yangtze's notorious floods have claimed more than one million lives in the past one hundred years. By creating a reservoir four hundred miles long, engineers believe the dam will bring an end to massive loss of life and property.

Professor R. Fuggle of the University of Cape Town, South Africa, and W.T. Smith, an independent American consultant, prepared a paper on the Three Gorges Dam for the World Commission on Dams. In it they discussed the devastating flood of 1998 that killed thousands and emphatically stated their opinion that, "It remains, however, the case that if Three Gorges had been in existence, the flood would have been a perfectly manageable event."[14]

Chinese engineers estimate that the hydropower station at the Three Gorges Dam will generate 85 billion kilowatt

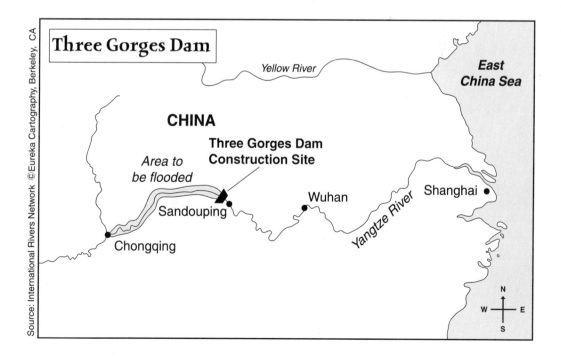

Source: International Rivers Network ©Eureka Cartography, Berkeley, CA

hours of electricity a year, one-eighth of the nation's total consumption. This amount is the equivalent of burning 25 million tons of crude oil, operating fifteen nuclear power plants, or burning 50 million tons of coal. The use of such a clean, reusable energy would definitely help to provide a less polluted living environment and will lessen China's dependence on expensive foreign oil imported from Russia. Presently, China spends several billion dollars annually on oil imports.

Harvesting the Forests

The Great Leap Forward needed still more from the Yangtze. One of the natural resources of the Yangtze River basin most needed to move industrialization forward was lumber. Along the mountainous middle reach, thick forests fed by the occasional over flooding of the river produced tall stands of timber. This was used for a myriad of wood products and for heating homes and running factories requiring high temperatures to produce their goods.

In keeping with the policies of the Great Leap Forward, large forests came under the new Ministry of Forestry in the early 1950s. With a total area of 3.8 million square miles, 760,000 of which is in the Yangtze River basin, China remains a country with extensive areas of natural and planted forests, about 17 percent of total land use. These forests are in huge demand by a population that continues to grow in size and affluence.

The densest forests of China, those within the upper and middle reaches, were designated to fulfill growing industrial needs for construction lumber and a variety of wood products needed by factories. These products include heavy shipping containers, cardboard boxes for foods, household cleaning products, paper bags, furniture, floors, computer paper, wrapping paper, and resins for paints and lacquers. Much of the lumber also energized housing construction allowing many families for the first time to move into well-constructed wooden homes instead of the traditional homes that lasted only a few years because they were built of materials such as bamboo, woven straw, and dried mud.

The Yangtze and its tributaries were called upon to transport millions of logs downriver to hundreds of lumber mills. Logs were chained together to form flotillas

Hydraulic Ship Lifts

One of the biggest engineering challenges facing the designers of the Three Gorges Dam is the requirement to provide some way to allow large ships to negotiate the dam on their way up and down the river. The requirement stipulated that cargo ships up to ten thousand tons had to be able to traverse the six-hundred-foot change in elevation. Furthermore, to ensure that the immense industrial city of Chongqing would continue to thrive, government officials insisted that at least five thousand ships a year must be able to negotiate the mammoth dam.

Engineers designed a two-lane five-step lock system on the north bank to lift or lower two vessels simultaneously. The principle is to move the ships up or down in a five-step sequence, each step increasing or decreasing the ship's elevation by roughly 120 feet. In keeping with the scale of the world's largest dam, these locks will be the largest in the world when operational. Each lock is a massive 910 feet long by 110 feet wide with a minimum water depth of sixteen feet. The pair of steel gates at each lock is 110 feet wide and 128 feet tall and each one of the pair weighs nine hundred tons. Because of the massive size and weight of the gates, all are operated by hydraulic cylinder hoists. It is estimated that it will take about three hours to pass one large cargo ship through the five locks.

Excavating for the two sets of locks was as extraordinary as the locks themselves. Fifty-two million cubic yards of rock was blasted from the side of the river. There are cut slopes close to six hundred feet tall. The stability of the locks relies on rock strength, augmented in places by rock bolting, tendons, and massive amounts of concrete.

To accommodate smaller vessels through the dam more quickly without using the very expensive five-stage locks, a ship elevator is being constructed on the opposite bank. It consists of a ship container, 390 feet long, 110 feet wide, and 16 feet deep. With the assistance of massive concrete counterbalances, this elevator will be capable of lifting vessels up to three thousand tons in a single vertical lift.

Six mill workers reposition a jammed log on the Yangtze. Loggers depend on the river to transport lumber to mills.

stretching hundreds of yards and marshaled downriver to mills where they were winched out of the water and sent to the saws.

As forests were cut for the production of commercial products, the deforested lands were cleared and converted into farmland for increasing food production. In some areas, a small percentage of trees was left standing on the fertile hills to provide shade along the Yangtze. The farmland, once cleared of most of the trees, was well suited for growing several major specialty crops such as tea, which had been a major export to England for many years. Local villagers recognized that tea could thrive planted beneath the canopies of tall trees, so they planted tea everywhere in the undergrowth of their community forests. Today tea is a main source of income for some villagers. Janet Sturgeon, reporting on this crop in 1998, commented that, "As villagers try to maintain the proper balance between sunlight and shade to produce abundant tea in the areas close to the villages, the 'forest' now looks like a tea plantation, with large trees scattered across the landscape."[15]

Some of the hilly areas where forest trees were completely removed were prime candidates for conversion to grain fields. Grains flourish best when grown on rich soil without any shade whatsoever. To accomplish this undertaking, plots of land were terraced where rice and other grains could prosper. These grain fields produced bumper crops because they benefited from the rich earth that had for thousands of years been forest land and from effective irrigation provided by nearby streams and rivers. These irrigated terraced fields outproduced the fields in the Yangtze Delta because they did not wash away during years of excessive flooding.

The close proximity of the new tea and grain fields to the river spurred the growth of food processing factories on the river's banks. The location of these factories facilitated the loading and transporting of finished food products to distant ports. Owners of other types of factories also recognized the benefits of convenient and inexpensive river transportation as well as the use of the river to eliminate factory waste products at virtually no cost.

Factories on the Yangtze

The Yangtze basin, which for eons had been the heart of China's agriculture, was poised to become equally important to the nation's industry. Following the Great Leap Forward during the decade of the 1960s, thousands of factories thirsting for billions of gallons of water sprang up along the river.

The banks of the Yangtze became prime real estate for industry. Factories depended more heavily on the Yangtze's water for processing products than did agriculture. Factories also depended upon the great river for the transportation of finished products to China's interior as well as to the nation's largest port city, Shanghai, for shipment to international ports. And as an added bonus, the river served as a conduit for removing effluent that resulted in the manufacturing process.

Factories on the river employed millions of workers in all sorts of jobs associated with the paper mills, steel mills, chemical factories, pharmaceutical plants, and textiles. Also employed were workers associated with leather dyeing, shipbuilding, and a multitude of manufacturing ranging from children's toys to small electronic equipment. The populations along the river viewed the industries as economic saviors because they provided jobs to urban dwellers and offered struggling farmers an alternative to working small plots of land. Of all the industries that grew up within the Yangtze basin, the two largest and most significant to China's economy were synthetic fertilizer and textile production.

The synthetic fertilizer industry began to boom when chemical plants sprang up along the Yangtze. Grain acreage increased following the deforestation of hills and the addition of new irrigated plots far from the river's silt-laden flow. These fields benefited from the use of synthetic fertilizers containing ammonia, chlorine, potassium, nitrogen, and phosphates used in the production of synthetic fertilizers. Thousands of tons annually produced yields of rice, wheat, soy, and safflower superior to the yields of these same crops grown organically in the Yangtze Delta. Prior to the existence of these chemical plants along the Yangtze, China imported all of its synthetic fertilizers from Russia at a tremendous cost. By manufacturing them, China was able to employ tens of thousands of workers and reduce its foreign debt at the same time.

The Yangtze also suited many of the needs of the textile industry. Textile factories require a tremendous volume of water for the cleaning of wool and cotton and for the production of dyes. Annually, billions of gallons of Yangtze water are drawn from the river, filtered to remove mud and silt, and piped into huge cleaning basins and dying vats. Following the actual production of the clothing articles, all are again subjected to a second immersion for a final cleaning to set the dyes and to shrink the material to the proper size. Following drying and packaging,

Located at the Yangtze River's mouth, Shanghai (pictured) has become the nation's largest port city.

cargo ships pick up the clothing destined for both local and foreign markets.

Within a decade, expanding factories hired millions of workers. Towns grew up that were completely dependent on factory production for jobs. The harnessing and development of the Yangtze also included building ports capable of loading and unloading the large cargo ships that supplied raw materials and carried away finished products. By the beginning of the 1990s, major Yangtze port cities such as Shanghai developed modern skylines that rivaled older established cosmopolitan port cities such as Hong Kong. Several Chinese business analysts highlighted the importance of the Yangtze in a 1992 article for *Fortune* magazine and one of them said:

> I'm very optimistic for China and Shanghai, especially if we adhere to our policy of opening up. We can catch up with or even surpass Hong Kong as China's leading business, industrial, and financial center. Why? Our industry is more comprehensive, diverse, and in many ways more advanced. Second, Shanghai sits at the mouth of the Yangtze River, a direct route to China's heartland.[16]

Over the past fifty years farmers and factory workers dependent in one way or another on the economy of the river experienced a rise in their standard of living. This rise is most easily seen in the reduction of hunger, improved primary health care, and reduction of infectious diseases. Since 1949 the average life span in China has risen from thirty-five years to the current seventy-one and the infant mortality rate has dropped during the same period from two hundred per one thousand to thirty-one per one thousand. Although many factors account for this impressive gain, no other natural resource has contributed more than the Yangtze.

As the nation's economy surged and millions living along the Yangtze experienced better health care and longer lives, signs slowly began to surface indicating that the river was paying a price for the new prosperity. Fishermen noticed it in smaller catches, delta farmers in flagging crop production, and families in chemical-related diseases. The Yangtze, it was becoming obvious to nearly everyone, was suffering in its attempt to meet the needs of a modern industrial nation.

4

· · · · · · · · · ·

A Threatened River

Within fifty years of taming and developing China's great lifeline, unmistakable symptoms of illness surfaced in the water of the middle and lower reaches of the river. What had for thousands of years appeared to be a river of limitless abundance was gradually but noticeably acquiring the look and smell of a suffering river. As farmers, fishermen, and scientists began closely examining the Yangtze, they discovered that the water quality had markedly declined. High concentrations of silt, factory pollution, and human waste from exploding populations clouded the water, reducing fish stocks and poisoning the drinking water of towns and cities along the river's banks.

The Great Leap Forward lasted just three years. It came to an end largely because the country experienced some of its worst droughts and floods in over one hundred years, thwarting any further attempts to control the Yangtze. Nonetheless, the Great Leap Forward's impact on the Yangtze was long-term and profound. The great environmental degradation of the river did not stop in 1961. Through the end of the millennium, China's continued efforts to industrialize the nation caused more pollution. By

Water pollution caused by industrial chemicals, riverside factories, and human waste threatens the Yangtze's health.

2000, despite the government's ambitious attempts to curb environmental damage and repair some of the damage from the previous three decades, the river was very ill.

The Yangtze basin had dramatically changed in just fifty years. Its population had quadrupled, large polluting factories occupied the banks of the river, several thousand dams were scattered throughout the basin, and fish disappeared at an alarming rate. Compared to the Yangtze basin just two generations before, very little remained unchanged.

The Population Explosion

The Chinese government that initiated the rapid move to industrialize the Yangtze River basin failed to anticipate the population explosion that would accompany it. The surge in population over the past fifty years along the middle and lower reaches is principally the result of the construction of factories that attracted large populations of workers. Secondly, the dams throughout the Yangtze River basin, which now exceed seven thousand in number, have provided enough flood control to allow more farmers to cultivate more acres of land. The dams have also produced enough electricity to light up cities that act as a beacon to peasants in rural villages. Everywhere along the Yangtze, cities are crowded and roads clogged with truck and automobile traffic.

Although no census had ever been taken in China prior to the 1949 revolution, world governments knew that China's population was the world's largest. For the purpose of economic planning, the first modern census, taken in 1952, reported the population of China to be 574 million, 100 million of whom lived within the Yangtze River basin. Less than fifty years later, the 2000 census reported the population of China had exploded to 1.3 billion, more than doubling. Even more astounding was the population increase of the Yangtze River basin, which quadrupled to a staggering 400 million.

An example of what has occurred along the Yangtze can be found in the city of Chongqing on the middle reach just up river from the Three Gorges. Prior to the twentieth century, Chongqing was one of hundreds of medium-sized cities throughout China. The city gradually increased in population during the last half of the century, but in 1997, it surged from a large city to the largest in China. According to journalist Lori Reese, this increase occurred when

Chongqing was granted special municipality status by Beijing to make it an economic magnet. The city got jurisdiction over 82,000 sq km of land that was once part of Sichuan [Szechwan], along with relaxed rules for foreign investment, in the hopes of building up a new industrial center. The idea was to decant economic development westward from the coastal areas—and to stanch the constant, eastward flow of rural migrants.[17]

This sudden population swell to forty million makes it the largest metropolitan center in China and the world as well. Modern Chongqing is an industrial city with thousands of factories producing iron and steel, chemicals, electrical power, automobiles, heavy construction equipment, ships, construction materials, textiles, foodstuffs, and pharmaceuticals.

Despite the best intentions of everyone along the Yangtze to respect the river, the changing demographics made fulfilling such intentions impossible. Ballooning populations stressed the river as billions of gallons of raw sewage poured into it. Industrial effluent posed an even more serious threat as chemicals, many of which are known carcinogens, pour into the Yangtze at a greater rate than human raw sewage. So serious became the condition of the water that many towns along the river ceased drawing the river water for household use.

Pollution

The explosions of population and factories have seriously polluted the Yangtze. Health officials contend that severe pollution exists in more than 52 percent of the Yangtze near urban areas. Roughly two-thirds of the river sections monitored in seven major river systems are severely contaminated with organic pollutants and a variety of industrial chemicals, all of which dramatically alter the quality of drinking water and adversely affect the wildlife of the river.

Vicki Harris, a pollution specialist at the University of Wisconsin's Sea Grant Institute in Green Bay, recently visited the Yangtze's largest cities on a scientific exchange program with the Beijing Institute for Environmental Studies.

Population Explosion Along the Yangtze

Nowhere in China has the population explosion been more in evidence than within the Yangtze basin. While the population in China, the highest in the world, has doubled over the past fifty years from 600 million to over 1.2 billion, the population of the Yangtze basin has quadrupled over the same period from 100 million to 400 million. Demographers who study population distributions wonder what makes the Yangtze so attractive to so many people.

Demographers point out that multiple reasons explain the population surge within the Yangtze basin. Part of the explanation is attributed to the normal increase in population, about 1.04 percent each year. This alone accounts for an annual increase of close to four million, but hardly enough to account for the enormous increase over the past fifty years.

More significant is the statistic that most of any nation's population clusters along the coastal regions and in fertile river valleys such as the Yangtze basin. These are the areas that support fishing, water for the irrigation of broad expanses of grain crops, and the exploitation of natural resources such as lumber and minerals. This observation is especially significant within the Yangtze River basin because the river and its seven hundred tributaries form such an extensive and invasive system that connects one-third of the entire nation. As a transportation and communication system, the Yangtze River binds more people together than any other river system in China.

Yet the most significant single explanation highlighted by demographers is the proliferation of industry. Since the Great Leap Forward, thousands of factories have settled along the river to take advantage of inexpensive transportation, unrestricted water usage, and unrestricted discharging of waste into the river. As factories multiplied, the demand for labor to staff them attracted millions willing to migrate from more remote regions for secure jobs and the cultural benefits of city life. In this regard, the nation as a whole is becoming more urban and less rural—one of the many characteristics of industrial nations.

A female Yangtze sturgeon is injected with hormones by fish farm workers to stimulate fertility. The sturgeon and other river wildlife are threatened by pollution.

Harris describes factories with open ditches that emptied into the Yangtze which, "Were filled with orange or yellow wastewater that was foaming before it even flowed into the river. . . . In less industrialized areas, sediment loads turned the water into a pinkish or yellowish chocolate-brown. Waters with more sewage looked more grayish."[18] As a result of these conditions, the people living along the Yangtze must either boil their water before drinking it or purchase bottled water.

The *People's Daily*, the official newspaper of the Chinese Communist Party, reported in August 2001, "According to an official report published in 1999, the amount of industrial waste and urban sewage discharged into the [Yangtze] river in that year totaled 20.7 billion tons, accounting for almost one-third of the country's total."[19] Of this tonnage, an estimated 90 percent comes from factories and 1.3 billion spewed from one industrial complex; Chongqing. Writer and world traveler Craig Neff, who toured the Yangtze in January 2001, reported:

> The smell of industry was overpowering . . . at the gargantuan commercial city of Chongqing to begin our four-day Yangtze cruise. Spend an afternoon choking on the acrid smog of Chongqing and you . . . come to understand why nine of the 10 cities in the world with the worst air and water pollution are Chinese.[20]

All of this toxic industrial material accumulates as it flows down the river becoming increasingly concentrated as it nears the delta. Loaded with ammonia, nitrogen, potassium permanganate, flammable petroleum byproducts, copper, and arsenic, only 42 percent of the river meets national drinking water standards according to United Nations estimates. Most of those areas that meet drinking water standards are along the river in the upper reach, leaving the delta to suffer the most. "Although the industries and townships along the Yangtze River Valley use 60 billion tons of water [a year] along the shore, it is difficult to find clean drinking water,"[21] said National People's Congress vice-chairman Zou Jianhua. A report issued by the Yangtze River Water Resources Authority concluded in 2002 that "Stretches of the 3,851 miles river are too polluted for human use."[22]

The Yangtze collects more than industrial chemicals as it flows to the sea, meandering through thousands of villages and dozens of cities with populations over one million. As the river sweeps past each one, it accumulates the untreated human sewage of all living there. Just fifty years ago, when the Yangtze basin was home to one quarter of its present population, the river effectively removed human waste sweeping it to the sea without raising concerns of bacterial contamination. Today, however, the population in the basin

The Demise of the Yangtze Sturgeon

The species of fish that has been brought to the brink of extinction due to pollution, over-fishing, and damming of the Yangtze is the Yangtze sturgeon, *Acipenser dabryanus*. This species is large and imposing as it swims. A mature sturgeon measures up to thirteen feet long and weighs over one thousand pounds, ranking it the biggest of all the twenty-seven species of sturgeon in the world and the biggest fish in the Yangtze River. This fish is considered a living fossil by ichthyologists because it dates back about 140 million years, almost to the same era of the dinosaur.

The Yangtze sturgeon is distributed mainly in the trunk tributaries of the Yangtze River and some coastal rivers. Between summer and autumn every year, they swim in schools upstream to the upper Yangtze River, even farther than Chongqing, where they spawn. After they are bred, they all swim downstream to grow in the Pacific Ocean. For a century or more these large animals have been hunted, not for their meat but for their eggs, called roe, that are packaged and sold as caviar at prices as high as sixty dollars an ounce. For many generations these fish were slaughtered for their eggs and dumped back into the rivers.

The Yangtze sturgeon is now on the list of protected animals by the Chinese government because its numbers in the Yangtze are now estimated to be about one hundred. According to the World Wildlife Federation, the sturgeon is disappearing because of severe pollution, habitat destruction, and by their inability to negotiate past dams where they migrate to spawn. Although the sturgeon is tightly protected along a 150-mile stretch, biologists are critical of this stretch because high concentrations of nitrogen from industry aggressively promote algae blooms. These blooms consume practically all the oxygen in parts of the Yangtze Delta, making it unfit for aquatic life. According to the article "China's Prosperity Turns Seas Toxic" in the *Baltimore Sun* newspaper on September 27, 2000, these scientists argue that oxygen levels are dangerously low in the entire area set aside as a sanctuary for the endangered Yangtze sturgeon.

is so large that the amount of raw sewage flowing daily into the Yangtze is a staggering 2 billion tons annually, roughly 1.3 billion gallons a day.

Erosion

The logging and paper industries flourished by cutting down expansive stands of forests. In Sichuan Province alone, forests that covered 20 percent of the land in the 1950s were reduced to a mere 9 percent by the end of the 1970s. Although these two industries experienced tremendous economic success in the short-term, scientists later recognized their long-term devastating effects. Lacking the deep roots of old mature trees, hillsides along the middle and lower reaches liquefied during the torrential downpours of the monsoon season allowing millions of tons of silt and mud to cascade into the Yangtze.

The decade of the 1990s served as a wake-up call to all residents along the river. As monsoon rains pummeled the Yangtze basin, residents faced the realities of the long-term effects of deforestation as landslides tore away valuable cropland along with entire villages and clotted the river with mountains of silt and mud. During the decade Sichuan Province alone experienced soil erosion exceeding sixty-two million acres.

The devastating floods of 1998 killed thousands, left millions homeless, and accounted for economic losses to industries and agriculture totaling $31 billion. Studies carried out by the United Nations Environmental Protection Agency (UNEP) following this devastating flood have found that siltation of the river reduces its water-carrying capacity, making it far more vulnerable to flooding.

The impact of erosion on the water-carrying capacity of the Yangtze and its tributaries can be seen throughout the river's basin. Many riverbeds were measured and found to be between two and fourteen feet higher as a result of siltation and soil from landslides. The hundreds of lakes that are sprinkled throughout the middle and lower reaches also fill with excess silt. The Dongting Lake is now filling up at the rate of about 1,677 million cubic yards of silt and soil annually. According to UNEP, the lake's bed has risen more than four feet in the last forty-five years. This loss of lakes area, which is critical for storing floodwaters, is very worrisome to limnologists. In 1949 the surface area of lakes along the Yangtze amounted to 6,640 square miles. By 1980 only 2,550 square miles remained, and in 1990 that figure shrank to 1,897 square miles. Studies in 1998 carried out by UNEP further stated:

> In the beginning of the 1950s, a total of 4,033 large and small lakes were found of which 759 were lakes with a surface area of more than one square mile. Of the 4,033 lakes, it is estimated that approximately 1,100 were lost in the last 45 years.[23]

Excessive silt and pollutants swirling through the Yangtze and its tributaries have degraded the only habitat available for hundreds of fish species. Fishermen noticed more empty nets than ever before. A once thriving fish industry was showing the symptoms of a sick and over-fished river.

Depleted Fish Stocks

The Yangtze is slowly becoming a giant cesspool that chokes off oxygen and vital nutrients to existing fish stocks. Pollution and excessive silt runoff coupled with over-fishing due to increased population demand have already severely reduced much of the Yangtze's aquatic life. Among the 140 species of fish in the river that were once commercially fished, by the 1990s only thirty were considered plentiful enough to qualify as "cash fish" and of those, only nine remain the targets for fishermen. The main nine are grass carp, black carp, silver carp, bighead, two species of bronze gudgeon, catfish, common carp, and yellow catfish.

The annual catch along the river has been in steady decline since the late 1950s when the total catch reached its peak at 427,000 tons in 1954. In 2002, however, according to the Chinese newspaper the *People's Daily*, "The figure dropped to around 100,000 tons in recent years."[24] Fishermen desperate to fill their nets have abandoned legal and traditional forms of line and net fishing in favor of dynamiting the river and scooping up the dead fish that float to the surface. Such reckless tactics are destructive to all species within the blast area. Imperiled are many protected species such as the nearly extinct baiji dolphins that were once revered in China as the goddesses of the Yangtze and the endangered twelve-foot-long Yangtze sturgeon, the population of which is estimated to be less than one hundred mature adults.

In the 1950s Lake Dongting's production of fish was twenty to thirty thousand tons annually. But during the 1980s, as silt began filling the lake and pollution poisoned fish stocks, the average fell to fifteen thousand tons. Hilsa herring of the Yangtze River also declined dramatically. Herring used to reach an annual output of over fifteen hundred tons in the 1970s, but this breed of fish has now almost completely disappeared here. Ao xie, a special breed of crab which lives around the mouth of the Yangtze River, faces the same fate. In 1981 the annual output of these crabs was seventy-two tons; by the 1990s the number had been reduced to only two tons.

Some of this extraordinary loss of fish is the result of mass fish kills along the banks of the Yangtze in the lower reach. Tons of fish that once might have been hauled aboard fishing boats are now found floating along riverbanks in one large heap. The fish cannot be eaten because they have died as a result of highly concentrated chemical pollution. According to the analysis of the water, metal elements such as copper, zinc, and chromium are poisoning the fish. Much of the pollution is washed downriver but, unfortunately for the fish, the industrial city of Shanghai, located on the Pacific coast, cannot flush its industrial pollution out to sea during periods of high tide or during storms that back up the natural flow of the river.

Excessive pollutants and overfishing degrade the habitat of species like Yangtze River dolphins. Today, less than one hundred such dolphins remain.

The Dilemma of Dams

Following the early successes of the many dams on the Yangtze, the Chinese government heavily promoted dam and reservoir construction, equating river flow diversions and hydroelectricity generation with an improved quality of life—and in one sense, it was true.

Unfortunately, by the decade of the 1990s the benefits that might have accrued from a few hundred dams were quickly overshadowed by a stampede to build more. Today there are more than seven thousand dams taller than fifty feet within the Yangtze River basin. Evidence of the last forty years shows these dams have created major problems along the river for the people as well as the environment. Of greatest concern to biologists is the effect these dams have of slowing down the natural flow of the river and the barriers they create for migrating fish stocks.

Since the earliest settlements along the river's banks, the Yangtze has been used as a sewer to carry all human waste and garbage to the sea. The annual summer monsoons once guaranteed a thorough cleansing of pollutants from the

A small river town sits below a new, modern city on higher ground. Once completed, the Three Gorges Dam will submerge towns like this one and displace over one million people.

river, allowing it to maintain a healthy and balanced habitat. As more dams were constructed to control the occasional large flood, the natural cleansing action was reduced causing more pollutants to remain in the river to the detriment of all biota. This condition is already evident in many of the tributaries of the Yangtze, and when the Three Gorges Dam is completed in 2008 limnologists predict that the concentration will become even more apparent.

Fish are one of many victims of the dams, some of which act as complete barriers to annual fish migrations. The fish stocks inhabiting much of the lower and middle reaches are dependent upon the lakes, especially Dongting within the lower reach, as breeding areas. Once the fry hatch and are large enough, many begin their migration from the lakes upriver where they will find plentiful supplies of food and room to mature. According to a biologist working for the Chinese government:

> Due to its advantageous geographical position and capacity in regulating the river flow, Dongting Lake acts as a key player in the river-lake ecological system and is an important base to replenish the colonies of many economic fishes in the Yangtze River. It is also an important freshwater fish production base.[25]

As millions of young fish make their ways up the Yangtze and its hundreds of tributaries, many are prevented from swimming beyond some of the larger dams. Unable to migrate, they turn back downriver where the competition for food is so great that they face starvation. As the populations of young fry dwindle, fewer survive to return to the lakes for breeding later in their lives. This loss in turn affects other species that feed on them and their fry, which throws the entire food cycle out of balance.

Cultural Disruptions

The damming of the Yangtze has created problems for people as well as fish. The construction of the Danjiangkou Dam displaced an estimated two hundred thousand villagers by the time the reservoir flooded tens of thousands of acres that had been farm land and hillside villages. This same displacement occurred to a lesser degree at the smaller dams, and by the 1980s Chinese ministers estimated a total of four hundred thousand Chinese had been forced to relocate far from their ancestral homes.

The construction of the Three Gorges Dam is already having an even greater cultural impact. Many disruptions have already occurred and government estimates indicate that the reservoir, once filled, will submerge 137 cities and towns, 1,300 factories, 1,100 villages, 4,000 hospitals and clinics, 40,000 grave sites and at least 178 garbage dumps containing 2.8 million tons of trash. Government estimates say 1.2 million people will be resettled and that new land is being provided for 300,000 farmers. Some observers say the government may be underestimating by as many as 700,000 the number of people who actually will be relocated.

Such an unfortunate loss of farmland, much of which has been tilled by the same Chinese families for centuries, will be particularly upsetting to those who live in the Three Gorges. According to Dr. John Byrne, director of the University of Delaware's Center for Energy and Environmental Policy, "One of the tragedies of this [project], if just from a regional standpoint, is that the land that is going to be flooded is some of the most fertile in China. The land to where the population is to be relocated is much less fertile."[26]

Archaeologists and historians have also joined to protest the dam. Its massive reservoir will submerge many of China's archaeological treasures that will be forever lost beneath six hundred feet of water. Teams are currently feverishly at work attempting to preserve some aspects of China's long and illustrious history along the river. Archaeologists and historians have estimated nearly thirteen hundred important sites will disappear before their artifacts can be recovered. Most irreplaceable, according to some experts, are remnants of the homeland of the Ba, who settled in the region about four thousand years ago. A former curator at Beijing's National Museum of Chinese History describes the area as "the last and best place to study Ba culture."[27]

The city of Fengdu is one of the most culturally interesting cities earmarked for a watery grave. Revered by the Chinese as the City of Ghosts, this fabled town, which sits on the north bank of the river, is a favorite stopping place for Chinese tourists visiting the temple erected to the gods of the underworld. In return for the city, the government promised to relocate the city on higher ground and to build a shopping center and a cultural museum. Townspeople, however, complain that instead of receiving these two buildings, they got a new hotel they did not want.

The hanging bridge at Fengdu's City of Ghosts marks the level water will rise to after the Three Gorges Dam is done.

Complaints such as this one and many others, prompted by changes on the Yangtze, can be heard up and down the river. Great environmental and cultural risks were taken to move China into the technology revolution of the twenty-first century in order to keep pace with industrial giants the likes of Japan, America, and several European powerhouses.

To a very great degree, the Great Leap worked as is witnessed by the peoples' noticeable increase in their quality of life. Yet the cost has been very high; the Yangtze now suffers from forty years of exploitation. But the river's present condition does not mean that it faces irrevocable harm. On the contrary, as the new century dawns, many scientists and environmental groups, both within and without China, are feverishly working to restore the river to a closer likeness of its former vitality.

5

The Yangtze in the Twenty-First Century

The Yangtze has awakened to the realities of modern technology. Despite the best of intentions to alter the river for the betterment of life in China, the dragon was delivered gravely ill to the doorstep of the new century. The task now faced by the Chinese and their leaders is to devise a long-term strategy to rescue China's most revered river before irreversible damage occurs. One valuable lesson over the past half-century was learned however; the river's ecological balance must be restored for the sake of its exotic wildlife and for the well-being of its people.

Reforesting

The greatest injury inflicted on the Yangtze that impacted people along its banks was deforestation. Following three decades of unusually devastating floods and erosion of hillsides during the monsoon rains, China moved boldly in 1998 to place a ban on logging and initiated plans to start a nationwide forest conservation project. The $2.5 billion plan, which is China's largest natural conservation project in history, will turn a million lumberjacks into tree-planters in the next several years to stabilize the hillsides against continued erosion.

The reforestation project plans to restore natural forests, grasslands, and other key habitats in the upper and middle reaches of the Yangtze basin. Since 1998, satellite surveys of Yunnan Province, Sichuan Province, and Chongqing municipality show signs that the ecology in the river basin

Saving the Forests

Reforesting is one of the government's highest priorities in controlling destructive floods and water pollution. The campaign to replant millions of acres of hillsides bordering the Yangtze and its tributaries combined with placing a ban on any further logging in the near-term is the government's solution. To achieve this outcome, each province within the upper and middle reaches of the river is implementing its own laws and policies.

Qinghai Province has taken the lead building a 380,000-acre forest belt along the upper Yangtze River over the past decade. Qinghai is located in some of the highest mountains in China where low temperatures and a harsh climate make for small but hearty forests. To protect the forests close to the river's source, the province began building a forest belt in 1989 to raise the forest coverage along the river.

Sichuan Province, also situated along the upper Yangtze River, started a pilot project in 1998 aimed to protect natural forest and return farmland to tall trees. The project has resulted in the recovery of vegetation and curbed the trend of soil erosion. Provincial leaders encouraged by the results of the reforestation program point out that ecological protection should be further emphasized and that the government ought to give this project preferential status. They suggest that in places with abundant rainfall, like the southern part of the country, efforts should be made to speed up returning farmland to vegetation.

Reforestation is of particular concern around the massive industrial city of Chongqing. A reforestation project, funded by the German government, is progressing smoothly and, according to local officials, has planted twenty-five thousand acres of trees along the Chongqing section of the river. The German government has been funding two Chinese cities every year since 1991 to help to improve the environment. The objective of the Chongqing reforestation project is to provide seventy-five thousand acres of trees by 2007 when it will be completed.

has started to improve. Erosion in the river basin has dropped visibly from 1.5 billion tons per year to 1.34 billion tons per year in 2002, down 11 percent. The reforestation area on the middle and upper banks of the Yangtze River has increased from 20 to 25 percent over the same period. In Yunnan Province, nearly a half million acres of land has been replanted raising the reforestation rate from 17 to 32 percent. Long-term objectives call for returning all cultivated slopes to forest or pasture within thirty to fifty years. They further call for the return of 22 million acres on very steep slopes, greater than twenty-five degrees, to forest or pasture by the year 2010.

From the beginning, the project to rehabilitate this watershed has also sought to incorporate indigenous knowledge of the local villagers. Their knowledge of medicinal plants has played an important role in the conservation of biodiversity and in practices of forest management by integrating various local gardening techniques. Because the collection and cultivation of plants for herbal medicines are important sources of income for many people, the cultivation of these plants at the base of trees is encouraged along with the planting of the trees. Growing herbs encourages farmers to respect the entire environment and to participate in ecological conservation, which in turn increases the economic return from the reforestation investment.

Wang Zhibao, director of China's State Forestry Bureau, understands that reforestation will not be completed overnight. Just because the government initiated a ban on logging along the river and implemented a large-scale reforestation project does not mean the erosion problem is over. As he said in a 2002 interview, "This may sound like a quick fix-all but, this plan will require 'generations and generations' to undo decades of environmental abuse. These problems cannot be solved in a short period of time"[28]

Controlling Water Pollution

Untreated industrial and human sewage is as much a problem as soil erosion. According to government officials, pollution of the Yangtze is getting worse. An official government report published in 2000 reported that the amount of industrial waste and human sewage discharged into the river that year totaled 20.7 billion tons, one-third of the country's total. Chinese officials recognize the need to cleanse the river and attach great importance to reducing the pollution by industries along the river. According to the *People's Daily* newspaper, "All the large factories have adopted substantial measures to minimize their discharge of waste into the country's largest river."[29]

According to the same source, "The participants [factory managers] agreed that the central government's plan to further strengthen water conservancy facilities in the Yangtze River area will promote environmental protection in an orderly manner."[30] The factory managers published a common declaration urging all industries in the area to abide by the environmental laws and regulations and to adopt substantial steps to protect the water quality of the Yangtze.

It is also imperative that government reduce the volume of untreated human waste that pollutes the river with high concentrations of toxic coliform bacteria. To meet this objective, a few large cities mix a disinfectant chemical called chlorine into the sewer pipes. A new and better technology that uses ultraviolet light to disinfect organic waste was more recently introduced. This disinfection process is championed by environmentalists because it has the advantage over the chlorine process of not introducing any chemicals into the river. Government officials hope that the ultraviolet process will eventually be used throughout the Yangtze basin.

In December 2001 the site chosen for construction of the first modern ultraviolet light sewage treatment plant was the most polluted spot along the river at the metropolis of Chongqing. The plant is designed to handle eleven million gallons daily. This ultraviolet light system will disinfect the wastewater and thus make a significant contribution to reducing pollution of the waters of the Yangtze. Five more ultraviolet light plants are scheduled that will have a combined capacity of an additional 34 million gallons a day.

Cleansing the Three Gorges

One of the major environmental concerns of opponents to the Three Gorges Dam is the mountain of hazardous waste that has been accumulating on the hillsides along the gorge. For generations this area has been used as a dump site, accumulating millions of tons of solid garbage and an equal tonnage of chemical effluent. The people counted on the natural flow and occasional flooding to flush out some of this debris. But when the dam is built, it will create the world's largest manmade lake, eliminating the annual flushing action.

In response to concerns about this mass of toxic garbage, a major cleanup of the 150-mile stretch of the river is underway. Failure to do so would mean that most of the debris would be forever trapped behind the dam, poisoning the four-hundred-mile reservoir for generations and possibly causing the extermination of all wildlife in the region.

By investing large sums of money, the Chinese government has undertaken to clean up the gorges and to construct water and garbage treatment facilities to prevent any further accumulation of hazardous materials. Officials say factories that will be submerged will be torn down and their sites scrubbed clean of pollutants. Paper and plastic are to be picked out of landfills and burned, while other trash will be carted to higher ground.

According to Guo Shuyan, director of the massive cleanup campaign, in an interview in 2002, all work "will be accomplished by the end of this year. Of the 788 factories to be removed, 664 have already been resettled. However, 96% of the firms that will be closed are in the process of bankruptcy clearance. Hubei [Province] and Chongqing will finish the work of cleaning the reservoir bed by the end of this year and are ready for inspection by the central government by March of next year."[31]

Guo Shuyan further indicates that technical standards have been well defined for the thorough removal of all garbage and solid waste from lands that will be submerged. Training has been offered to relevant staff and the funds for this work have been appropriated. Chongqing has already built nineteen sewage and five garbage disposal centers and Hubei has started construction on four sewage and four garbage disposal centers that are expected to be finished before June 2003.

Some of the money is also earmarked to upgrade the pollution control facilities of factories. By 2010 the Chinese government promises the construction of 146 wastewater disposal centers and 161 garbage treatment plants in cities and towns around the reservoir. New emission standards for factories have also been defined. According to Liu Qifeng with the State Environmental Protection Administration, "Paper mills, fertilizer plants, wine breweries, mines and other heavy-polluters will be closed if they fail to meet the pollutant emission standards set by the state."[32]

Paper and plastic debris like this must be removed from low-lying landfills before the Three Gorges Dam inundates a 150-mile stretch of river valley.

Rejuvenating Fish Stocks

Rejuvenating the declining fish stocks in the Yangtze has been a high priority second only to the cleanup of the river. Ichthyologists, biologists who specialize in fish, have made several other recommendations to the Chinese government that will hasten the return of the river's aquatic life, the most important of which is to restrict fishing.

China's government announced in 2001 that "China will ban fishing on its longest river, the Yangtze, from February to June next year to protect marine resources endangered by over-fishing."[33] This proclamation marks the beginning of a campaign to restore fish stocks to healthy levels. The city of Nanjing in the lower reach of the Yangtze basin is the first area to observe a three-month fishing ban on the river from April 1 through July l. Other cities have also been assigned fishing ban periods as has the huge Lake Dongting. Everyone concerned with increasing the river's fish stocks is in agreement that these bans will contribute to the sustainability of all species.

Government officials understand that such laws, which ban fishing during its peak season, will cost fishermen a substantial amount of their income. In Nanjing alone there are nearly four hundred registered fishing boats and fifteen hundred fishermen. To compensate for the losses of the fishing community, the government has offered a monthly subsidy of roughly twenty-five dollars to each fisherman. Those who depend on fishing for a living say they understand why the ban has been put in place and hope it will lead to a better harvest in the future.

In addition to the ban, China has further moved to protect Yangtze fish by revoking the right of foreign fishing boats to fish on the river. Under a recent accord, South Korean fishing boats, which had been allowed to catch a maximum of 13,600 tons of blue crab in the lower part of the Yangtze River, will no longer be allowed to enter the fishing grounds after 2003.

The government also has recently invested in fish farms, artificial breeding programs for fish. A technical breakthrough has made it possible to breed temperate zone fish on a large scale in subtropical tributaries of the Yangtze in southeast China. One of the hardier fish, a species of freshwater flounder, has adapted well to the warmer tributaries, demonstrates a high survival rate, and produces a large number of fry every year. To date, six million fry, which have an estimated commercial value of about $8.5 million, have been bred in fish farms.

To further assist the flagging fishing industry, the World Wildlife Federation has helped fish farmers develop alternative livelihoods while living in harmony with the wetlands. They are now working in what are termed "wetland industries" that do not harm the environment. Environmentalists working for the World Wildlife Federation have hopes that fish farmers' incomes will increase in a variety of wetland industries. One of these new industries involves raising fish within protective floating cages and another involves planting crops in the wetlands. A third one, very different from the others, involves ecotourism projects that provide boat excursions for tourists interested in the river's habitat.

Soft Solutions to Dams

One opinion that is becoming increasingly common within the scientific community and the environmental movement is that, with more than seven thousand dams taller than fifty feet, the Yangtze already has too many dams. To address the needs to control the occasional massive flash flood and to generate more electricity, other so-called "soft solutions" are recommended as alternatives to steel and concrete dams.

One soft solution to flood control highlights flood plain management. It has been concluded that agricultural encroachment onto lakebeds and other wetlands in the Yangtze Delta has reduced natural storage areas. A recommendation has been made to relocate upwards of a million people, some onto higher land in the same vicinity, others to completely new settlements away from the flood plain. A second recommendation is to dredge millions of tons of silt out of the major Yangtze channels along the delta which will provide more storage capacity during unusually high floods. According to limnologist Ye Lou,

Wooden Chopsticks—A Thing of the Past?

Are the Chinese willing to depart from an age-old tradition to support the current ban on logging? To save trees, environmentalists in China are campaigning to significantly reduce the number of disposable wooden chopsticks used in the country. Chopsticks, called *kuai-zi*, are two long, thin, usually tapered pieces of wood used deftly like pincers to pick up food. It is widely believed that five thousand years ago the Chinese cooked their food in large pots which held heat for a long time, and that eaters broke twigs off trees to retrieve the food. By 400 B.C., because of a large population and dwindling resources, food was chopped into small pieces so it could be cooked rapidly to conserve fuel. The pieces of food were small enough that they no longer required knives at the dinner table, and thus, chopsticks became the standard utensils.

Although most chopsticks are fairly simple, some are quite artistic. Chopsticks are sometimes made of lacquered wood and covered with artwork. Truly elegant chopsticks might be made of gold and embossed in silver with Chinese calligraphy. Artisans also combine various hardwoods and metal to create distinctive designs. Estimates from Chinese sources report that the current number of chopsticks used annually is about 45 billion pairs.

Traditionally, chopsticks are carved from bamboo, cedar, sandalwood, teak, or pine. Sources contend that somewhere between 3 and 6 million trees are sacrificed each year in chopstick manufacturing, a number that must be reduced in compliance with the current ban of logging.

Efforts toward phasing out disposable wooden chopsticks are paying off. Many people now carry stainless steel chopsticks that can be washed and reused after eating. In February 2001 hundreds of restaurants in major population centers agreed to begin reusing chopsticks, while in Shanghai a tax on disposable wooden chopsticks took effect in October 2000. China's Ministry of Finance is said to be working on enacting similar legislation nationwide.

Due to years of farmland reclamation from the lakes along the river, the lake surface and water resources have rapidly shrunk. As a result, the role of the lakes in flood-prevention has decreased and the overall ecological environment in the Yangtze River valley has been damaged. So far, about 50 lakes along the river have been cut off from the river.[34]

Prior to the dam-building mania that followed the 1949 revolution, the principal strategy of flood control was the construction of many soft solution projects such as thousands of miles of dykes, levees, retention basins, diversion ditches, and pumping schemes to divert water. During the devastating flood of 1998, millions of workers fought valiantly to increase the height of levees with remarkable success. Although the river inundated many towns and

Coal manufacturing plants like this one operate to help decrease China's reliance on hydroelectricity.

cities, the system of dykes and levees saved many others. The World Wildlife Federation has recommended the continuation of these soft solutions as a more viable and less environmentally destructive strategy than large dams.

These same scientists and environmentalists from around the world also recommend soft solutions to the electricity shortage. Instead of depending on large dams to generate hydroelectricity, they recommend conventional sources of energy and conversion systems that burn coal, use nuclear fuels, or burn natural gas in turbine converters. Scientists studying China's situation also recommend adding capacity to existing hydroelectric dams as an option for increasing the energy supply. Some of these options may be more cost-effective than others. According to professor R. Fuggle and W.T. Smith, "A combined cycle gas turbine costs about $650 per kilowatt, roughly 15 to 40 per cent of the cost per kilowatt for Three Gorges."[35] They also point out that existing hydropower facilities on the Yangtze were primarily built for average load energy production. Experts in hydroelectricity contend that these existing facilities can be adapted to provide two to three times the present output.

Also recommended are the use of unconventional sources of electricity such as wind power, photovoltaic (solar) power, fuel cell technology that requires hydrogen-rich gases, and using energy from other fossil fuel plants. Proponents of these incipient power generation technologies admit that their impact would be small in China because such systems are still relatively small. Nonetheless, supporters of these new technologies insist that the more they are used, the more quickly they will move from the unconventional category to the conventional.

Epilogue: A Great Leap Forward or Backward?

Some say the Giant Leap Forward's rush to propel China into competition with industrialized nations has been a bitter pill for the Yangtze River. Asked to shoulder a major burden of responsibility, China's most imposing river has spurred a great debate over the prudence and impact of such a strategy. One faction acknowledges the burden placed on the river yet believes the sacrifice will have long-term benefits for all of China. The other, however, believes the rush was a poorly conceived strategy that has inflicted irreversible damage on the Yangtze and those dependent on its water. Which prediction will ultimately be fulfilled may not be known for many generations.

China has committed itself to two paths that may not be entirely compatible: rapid economic development as a means to prosperity, and environmental protection to ensure a sustainable economy. If these events were occurring in a smaller country, fewer within the international community would take notice. But when 1.3 billion people suddenly change their way of life, global complaints can be anticipated.

The group expressing pessimism about China's long-term policies concerning the use of the Yangtze principally represents scientists and environmentalists outside of China. The overwhelming majority of this group believe that Chinese officials have engaged in reckless exploitation of the river—too many dams, too much deforestation, too few waste treatment plants, and a general lack of environmental concern. This multi-national group, which is opposed to any further development along the basin, warns that the major obstacle preventing the revitalization of the river is lack of money. China, they correctly point out, is still a poor country struggling to compete with fully developed wealthy

Workers wave flags to celebrate the successful damming of a Yangtze River canal in southwestern China in 2002.

industrial nations. Many of the real solutions such as replanting forests, providing job alternatives to lumbering and polluting industries, replacing old facilities with clean technology, and adding hundreds of needed water treatment plants are infuriatingly long-term in a country that is bursting to be prosperous immediately.

Optimism for the river's future is almost exclusively voiced by Chinese government officials through the one official Chinese newspaper, the *People's Daily*. Their view, expressed in numerous environmental articles, paints a bright future for the Yangtze River. They recognize there is much work to be done restoring the river's vitality and they fully expect that the river will recover as a result of new policies restricting pollution and rectifying earlier abuses of forests, overfishing, and dam construction.

Not all Chinese, however, are so confident about the river's future, but many are reluctant to voice their opinions. According to Dai Qing, an author who received a ten-month prison sentence and a lifelong ban against publishing in China for her criticism of the government's policies toward the Yangtze, commented in 2002, "Today, only 'positive reporting' about the Three Gorges Dam is allowed in China."[36]

At the national level, China has been passing new environmental regulations and reconstructing its governing and enforcement infrastructure at a rate that would make most governments look sluggish. Yet, despite China's rapidly evolving and complex network of environmental policies and laws designed to restore the Yangtze to good health, compliance with environmental regulations remains low. A popular expression along the Yangtze says about China's capital city Beijing, "The top has a policy, the bottom has a way around it."[37] This scofflaw attitude was noted by one American journalist who recently observed flagrant violations of laws prohibiting the pollution of the Yangtze:

As the tourist boats ply the river, packed to the gills with passengers admiring the view, many blithely toss their cigarettes, styrofoam dinner boxes and other wrappers overboard. The boat disgorges all the collective sewage from the three-day trip into the Yangtze before dropping its passengers in the city of Wuhan.[38]

There's an old Chinese saying: "Once the last tree is cut and the last river poisoned, you will find you cannot eat your money."[39] Standing at the threshold of the twenty-first century, this old Chinese proverb might be prophetic. The people of China face the challenge of balancing the pace of economic development with the need to protect the environment. It is likely that the Yangtze will continue to experience serious pollution as well as other environmental problems during the early part of this century. Yet China is capable of meeting both economic and environmental goals by implementing a sustainable development strategy, improving public awareness in the area of environmental protection, vigorously enforcing relevant laws, applying new technologies, and inviting technical assistance from more advanced nations.

Notes

· · · · · · · ·

Introduction: A Dragon of a River

1. Quoted in *Imperial Tours,* "The Three Gorges," March 2001. www.imperialtours.net.

Chapter 1: Carver of Mountains

2. Quoted in *Imperial Tours,* "The Three Gorges."
3. Quoted in Lyman P. van Slyke, *Yangtze: Nature, History and the River.* New York: Addison-Wesley, 1988, p. 8.

Chapter 2: China's Lifeline

4. Quoted in *Public Broadcasting Service,* "Great Wall Across the Yangtze." www.pbs.org.
5. Kwang-Chih Chang, *The Archaeology of Ancient China.* New Haven: Yale University Press, 1987, p. 86.
6. Chang, *The Archaeology of Ancient China,* p. 177.
7. Chang, *The Archaeology of Ancient China,* p. 177.
8. Josh Goldman, "Aquaculture, Widely Recognized to Be a Reliable and Clean Source of Fish Protein," *Fins Technology.* www.finstechnology.com.
9. Chang, *The Archaeology of Ancient China,* p. 203.
10. Quoted in van Slyke, *Yangtze,* p. 81.
11. Quoted in van Slyke, *Yangtze,* p. 56.
12. Carolyn Walker, Ruth Lor Malloy, Robert Shipley, and Fu Kailin, *On Leaving Bai Di Cheng:The Culture of China's Yangzi Gorges.* Toronto: NC Press, 1993, page 202.

Chapter 3: Taming and Developing the Dragon

13. Quoted in van Slyke, *Yangtze,* p. 79.
14. R. Fuggle and W.T. Smith, "Experience with Dams in Water and Energy Resource: Development in the People's Republic Of China," *World Commission on Dams,* November 2000. www.damsreport.org.

15. Janet Sturgeon, "State Policies, Ethnic Identity, and Forests in China and Thailand," *Mountain Forum,* 1998. www.mtnforum.org.

16. Bao Shuping, Wei Wen Yuan, Duan Yongji et al., "Pacific Rim/Cover Stories: Leaders Look at the Next Decade," *Fortune,* October 5, 1992, p. 64.

Chapter 4: A Threatened River

17. Lori Reese, "Chongqing: A Floating Population," *Time Asia,* vol. 154, no. 12, September 27, 1999, p. 106.

18. Quoted in Corliss Karasov, "On a Different Scale: Putting China's Environmental Crisis in Perspective," *Environmental Health Perspectives,* vol. 108, no. 10, October 2000, p. 57.

19. *People's Daily,* "China Curbs Industrial Pollution Along Yangtze River," August 16, 2001. http://english.peopledaily.com.

20. Craig Neff, "Taming the Dragon," *Via,* January 2001. www.viamagazine.com.

21. Quoted in *Three Gorges Probe,* "Study Puts Price on Ecological Ruin," December 31, 2001. www.threegorgesprobe.org.

22. Quoted in Robin Nicholson, "Yangtze River Pollution at Dangerous Levels," *New Scientist,* January 30, 2002, p. 58.

23. Quoted in *Green Nature,* "The Yangtze River and Flood Reduction Plans," October 12, 2001. http://greennature.com.

24. Quoted in *People's Daily,* "China to Begin Fishing Ban on Lower Reaches of Yangtze in April," March 27, 2002. http://english.peopledaily.com.

25. Quoted in *China Environmental Protection,* "Three Gorges," May 2002. www.zhb.gov.

26. Quoted in Bruce Kennedy, "China's Three Gorges Dam," *CNN.com,* 2001. www.cnn.com.

27. Quoted in Kennedy, "China's Three Gorges Dam."

Chapter 5: The Yangtze in the Twenty-First Century

28. Quoted in *University of Arkansas Little Rock,* "Reforesting the Yangtze River Watershed: The Implications for China," October 2002. ww.ualr.edu.

29. *People's Daily,* "China Curbs Industrial Pollution along Yangtze River."

30. *People's Daily,* "China Curbs Industrial Pollution along Yangtze River."

31. Quoted in *China,* "Future Three Gorges Reservoir Bed to Be Cleaned," September 29, 2002. www.china.org.

32. Quoted in *People's Daily,* "Water Pollution in Three Gorges Dam Warned," November 2001. http://english.peopledaily.com.

33. *People's Daily,* "China to Impose Fishing Ban on Yangtze River," November 21, 2001. http://english.peopledaily.com.

34. Quoted in *China,* "Saving Aquatic Resources in the Yangtze River," May 2000. www.china.org.

35. Fuggle and Smith, "Experience with Dams in Water and Energy Resource: Development in the People's Republic of China."

Epilogue: A Great Leap Forward or Backward?

36. Quoted in *International Rivers Network,* "The River Dragon Has Come!," January 2002. www.irn.org

37. John Pomfret, "Yangtze Flood Jolts China's Land Policies," *Washington Post,* November 22, 1998.

38. Kari Huss, "The Yangtze's Collision Course—Where Nature Faces Off with Industry and the Human Species," *MSNBC News,* 1999. www.msnbc.com.

39. Quoted in *Green Peace,* "China: Executive Summary," February 2001. http://archive.greenpeace.org.

For Further Reading

Books

Thomas W. Blakiston, *Five Months on the Yang-tsze*. London: John Murray, 1862. An interesting source of information about preindustrial China, this book is one of the early works describing the Yangtze as well as the towns and people of the river. Its rich and enthusiastic text details the characteristics of the river and local customs.

Dai Qing, *The River Dragon Has Come! The Three Gorges Dam and the Fate of China's Yangtze River and Its People*. Trans. Ming Yi. Armonk, NY: M.E. Sharpe, 1998. A comprehensive collection of essays addressing the potential problems of constructing China's Three Gorges Dam. Of particular interest is the collection of accounts about the 1975 dam collapses in China, the cost of the human resettlement plans, the loss of archaeological treasures; and the accumulations of industrial and human waste in the reservoir.

Robert K. G. Temple, *The Genius of China: 3000 Years of Science, Discovery, and Invention*. Touchstone, 1986. A fascinating science history with hundreds of illustrations. It is chock full of fascinating scientific information about ancient Chinese science and technology.

Wang Chaosheng, *Farming and Weaving Pictures in Ancient China*. Beijing: China Agriculture Press, 1995. This book tells the story of ancient agriculture in China. One of its greatest features is its over four hundred ancient Chinese paintings depicting agriculture that answer many questions about how farming was practiced.

Works Consulted

Books

Kwang-Chih Chang, *The Archaeology of Ancient China*. New Haven, CT: Yale University Press, 1987. Chang's work remains one of the few comprehensive books on ancient Chinese cultures in the English language. This covers all of China with several chapters about the Yangtze River.

Jiang Liu, *Changjiang: The Longest River in China*. Beijing: Foreign Language Press, 1980. One of the few books that provides a history of the river prior to the construction of the Three Gorges Dam. It also includes some remarkably beautiful photographs of villages and nature along the river banks.

Robert Temple, *The Genius of China: 3,000 Years of Science, Discovery, and Invention*. New York: Simon and Schuster, 1986. The author of this book has accumulated the work of many scholars working on ancient Chinese technology. Aided by many illustrations, Temple provides an illuminating work that documents many Chinese inventions that predate the European discovery.

Lyman P. van Slyke, *Yangtze: Nature, History and the River*. New York: Addison-Wesley, 1988. This is one of the very few books written in English to present a comprehensive discussion and description of the Yangtze. It discusses the river's origins, history, physical attributes, and the lives of those living along its banks.

Carolyn Walker, Ruth Lor Malloy, Robert Shipley, and Fu Kailin, *On Leaving Bai Di Cheng: The Culture of China's Yangzi Gorges*. Toronto: NC Press, 1993. A compilation of notes written by four journalists who traveled by boat through the Three Gorges the year before construction began on the dam. It is informal, colorful, and filled with insights about the population living along the river.

Periodicals

Baltimore Sun, "China's Prosperity Turns Seas Toxic," September 27, 2000.

Hannah Beech, "Fengdu, From Sapporo to Surabaya/Fengdu, China: Troubled Waters," *Time International,* August 21, 2000.

Julie Chao, "Relocation for Giant Dam Inflames Chinese Peasants," *Palm Beach Post,* May 15, 2001.

Martin Fackler, "New Home for Yangtze's Goddesses," *Los Angeles Times,* July 21, 2002.

Corliss Karasov, "On a Different Scale: Putting China's Environmental Crisis in Perspective," *Environmental Health Perspectives,* vol. 108, no. 10, October 2000.

Robin Nicholson, "Yangtze River Pollution at Dangerous Levels," *New Scientist,* January 30, 2002.

John Pomfret, "Yangtze Flood Jolts China's Land Policies," *Washington Post,* November 22, 1998.

Lori Reese, "Chongqing: A Floating Population" *Time Asia,* vol. 154, no. 12, September 27, 1999.

Bao Shuping, Wei Wen Yuan, Duan Yongji et al., "Pacific Rim/Cover Stories: Leaders Look at the Next Decade," *Fortune,* October, 5, 1992.

Internet Sources

China, "Future Three Gorges Reservoir Bed to Be Cleaned," September 29, 2002. www.china.org.

——, "Saving Aquatic Resources in the Yangtze River," May 2000. www.china.org.

China Environmental Protection, "Three Gorges," May 2002. www.zhb.gov.

R. Fuggle and W.T. Smith, "Experience with Dams in Water and Energy Resource: Development in the People's Republic of China," *World Commission on Dams,* November 2000. www.damsreport.org.

Josh Goldman, "Aquaculture, Widely Recognized to Be a Reliable and Clean Source of Fish Protein," *Fins Technology.* www.finstechnology.com.

Green Nature, "The Yangtze River and Flood Reduction Plans," October 12, 2001. http://greennature.com.

Green Peace, "China: Executive Summary," February 2002. http://archive.greenpeace.org.

Kari Huss, "The Yangtze's Collision Course—Where Nature Faces Off with Industry and the Human Species," *MSNBC News*, 1999. www.msnbc.com.

Imperial Tours, "The Three Gorges." www.imperialtours.net

International Rivers Network, "The River Dragon Has Come!" January 2002. www.irn.org

Bruce Kennedy, "China's Three Gorges Dam," *CNN.com*, 2001. www.cnn.com.

Bill Moyers, "The History of Chinese in America: From American Revolution to Wen-ho Lee," *Committee of 100*, May 5, 2000. www.committee100.org.

Craig Neff, "Taming the Dragon," *Via*, January 2001. www.via-magazine.com.

Ron O'Callaghan, "Chinese Funerary Figures," *Asian Trade Arts & Antiques*. www.rugreview.com.

People's Daily, "China Curbs Industrial Pollution Along Yangtze River," August 16, 2001. http://english.peopledaily.com.

———, "China to Begin Fishing Ban on Lower Reaches of Yangtze in April," March 27, 2000. http://english.peopledaily.com.

———, "China to Impose Fishing Ban on Yangtze River," November 21, 2001. http://english.peopledaily.com.

———, "Water Pollution in Three Gorges Dam Warned," November 2001. http://english.peopledaily.com.

Public Broadcasting Service, "Great Wall Across the Yangtze." www.pbs.org.

Janet Sturgeon, "State Policies, Ethnic Identity, and Forests in China and Thailand," *Mountain Forum*, 1998. www.mtnforum.org.

Three Gorges Probe, "Study Puts Price on Ecological Ruin," December 31, 2001. www.threegorgesprobe.org.

University of Arkansas Little Rock, "Reforesting the Yangtze River Watershed: The Implications for China," October, 2002. www.ualr.edu.

Websites

China (www.china.org). Highlights events of interest occurring in China and provides stories that optimistically depict life and events in China.

China Environmental Protection (www.zhb.gov). An official website of the Chinese government that reports on a variety of environmental issues including current issues involving air, land, and water quality.

CNN.com (www.cnn.com). The CNN website is affiliated with the Cable News Network organization and it provides online national and international news.

Environmental News Network (www.enn.com). Provides educational information about environmental issues throughout the world. The website offers timely environmental news, live chats, interactive quizzes, daily feature stories, forums for debate, and a variety of audio and video programs.

Fins Technology (www.finstechnology.com). Provides information on fish farming, technologies, history, markets, and other information for people interested in the business of aquaculture.

Green Nature (http://greennature.com). A site dedicated to environmental causes: political, social, scientific, and cultural. It contains hundreds of websites and links that address environmental news around the world.

Green Peace (http://greenpeace.org). Green Peace is a global organization committed to active participation in protecting and preserving earth's biodiversity and environment. The website contains articles and links relevant to the preservation of the planet and its wildlife.

Imperial Tours (www.imperialtours.net). A commercial website providing information about tours of the Yangtze River.

International Rivers Network (www.irn.org). Provides articles on and links to international environmental and scientific groups working to protect their rivers and watersheds. Its charter is to halt destructive river development projects and to encourage equitable and sustainable methods of meeting needs for water, energy, and flood management.

MSNBC (www.msnbc.com). The Microsoft/National Broadcasting

Company Internet service that provides daily news headlines from around the world.

People's Daily (http://english.peopledaily.com). The website of China's official newspaper, updated daily with English translations of the newspaper's lead stories.

Public Broadcasting Service (PBS) (www.pbs.org). Provides written articles and accompanying photographs covering hundreds of educational topics that are also presented on the PBS television station. This website is an excellent and rich resource for researching pressing topics around the world.

Three Gorges Probe (www.threegorgesprobe.org). This website is dedicated to stopping the construction of the Three Gorges Dam. It contains a compelling number of articles written by scientists who have studied the project and provides dozens of photographs of the gorges as well as models of the dam. University of Arkansas Little Rock (www.ualr.edu). The central website for the University of Arkansas at Little Rock contains links to all campus activities as well as faculty and current research projects.

Via Magazine (www.viamagazine.com). Stories for travelers that highlight cities and locations around the globe.

World Commission on Dams (www.damsreport.org). A website dedicated to publishing reports on major dams throughout the world. It provides unbiased scientific information on dam construction and the impact of dams on populations and environments.

Index

Picture Credits

• • • • • • • • • • • • • • • • • • •

About the Author

James Barter received his undergraduate degree in history and classics at the University of California at Berkeley, followed by graduate studies in ancient history and archaeology at the University of Pennsylvania. Mr. Barter has taught history as well as Latin and Greek.

A Fulbright scholar at the American Academy in Rome, Mr. Barter worked on archaeological sites in and around the city as well as on sites in the Naples area. Mr. Barter also has worked and traveled extensively in Greece.

Mr. Barter currently lives in Rancho Santa Fe, California, with his seventeen-year-old daughter Kalista who is a senior at Torrey Pines High School, works as a soccer referee, excels at math, physics, and English, and daily mulls her options for college next year. Mr. Barter's older daughter, Tiffany, lives nearby with her husband Mike. Tiffany teaches violin and performs in classical music recitals.